LEVEL H

VOCABULARY

word meaning, pronunciation, prefixes, suffixes, synonyms, antonyms, and fun!

in Action

LOYOLA PRESS.

Chicago

LOYOLA PRESS.

3441 N. Ashland Avenue
Chicago, Illinois 60657
(800) 621-1008
www.loyolapress.com

Cover & Interior Art: Anni Betts
Cover Design: Judine O'Shea
Interior Design: Kathy Greenholdt and Joan Bledig

ISBN-10: 0-8294-2776-7

ISBN-13: 978-0-8294-2776-9

17 Hess 10 9 8 7 6

Contents

Pronunciation Key

This key shows the meanings of the abbreviations and symbols used throughout the book.

Some English words have more than one possible pronunciation. This book gives only one pronunciation per word, except when different pronunciations indicate different parts of speech. For example, when the word *relay* is used as a noun, it is pronounced rē´ lā; as a verb, the word is pronounced rə lā´.

Parts of Speech

adj.	adjective	*int.*	interjection	*prep.*	preposition
adv.	adverb	*n.*	noun	*part.*	participle
				v.	verb

Vowels

ā	tape	ə	about, circus	ôr	torn
a	map	ī	kite	oi	noise
âr	stare	i	win	ou	foul
ä	car, father	ō	toe	o͞o	soon
ē	meet	o	mop	o͝o	book
e	kept	ô	law	u	tug

Consonants

ch	check	ŋ	rang	y	yellow
g	girl	th	thimble	zh	treasure
j	jam	t̶h̶	that	sh	shelf

Stress

The accent mark follows the syllable receiving the major stress, such as in the word *plaster* (plas´ tər).

Pretest

This test contains some of the words you will find in this book. It will give you an idea of the kinds of words you will study. When you have completed all the chapters, the Posttest will measure what you have learned.

CHOOSING THE DEFINITIONS

Fill in the bubble next to the item that best defines the boldface word in each sentence.

1. The doctor's **diagnosis** was a relief to the whole family.
   a. instruction **b.** conclusion **c.** medicine **d.** conversation

2. We feel and look better when we practice good **hygiene** every day.
   a. house cleaning **b.** promptness **c.** personal health **d.** honesty

3. Noah was **despondent** when his best friend moved away.
   a. elated **b.** furious **c.** solitary **d.** depressed

4. The citizens committee turned the **dilapidated** warehouse into a recreation center.
   a. enormous **b.** stone **c.** abandoned **d.** ruined

5. The **glutton** at the banquet annoyed everyone.
   a. greedy eater **b.** long table **c.** main dish **d.** staff of waiters

6. An angry bear is a **ferocious** beast.
   a. savage **b.** playful **c.** strong **d.** clumsy

7. The desert is beautiful, but the afternoon sun may make us **swelter**.
   a. search for water **b.** get lost **c.** seek shelter **d.** suffer from heat

8. My friend and I leave notes for each other in a shallow **niche** in the stone wall.
   a. cavern **b.** hole **c.** glass box **d.** shelf

9. Mom said the loud music from the stereo was **intolerable**.
   a. pleasant **b.** unbearable **c.** exciting **d.** deafening

10. His friend's request caused a serious **dilemma** for Andy.
    a. illness **b.** expression **c.** choice **d.** crime

11. You can spread happiness by performing **random** acts of kindness.
    a. generous **b.** unplanned **c.** planned **d.** silent

12. **Famine** forced some immigrants to move to the United States.
    a. government **b.** persecution **c.** injustice **d.** starvation

13. The blue gill is the most **prevalent** fish in Eagle Lake.
  (a.) freshwater   (b.) common   (c.) poisonous   (d.) rare

14. Ever since that incident, Albert has held a **grudge** against Omar.
  (a.) resentment   (b.) kindness   (c.) sadness   (d.) indifference

15. Her **affinity** for animals may lead her to become a veterinarian.
  (a.) dislike   (b.) ownership   (c.) fondness   (d.) fear

16. Our class circulated a **petition** to keep the after-school program.
  (a.) chain letter   (b.) magazine   (c.) written request   (d.) survey

17. Even though Kwan speaks Chinese, she has trouble understanding her new friend's **dialect**.
  (a.) conversation   (b.) pronunciation   (c.) idea   (d.) picture

18. I like to sing, but I can never remember the **lyrics**.
  (a.) words   (b.) tunes   (c.) titles   (d.) keys

19. I dislike the artist's style, but I admire her **diligence**.
  (a.) imagination   (b.) skill   (c.) hard work   (d.) collection

20. After the power failure, we had to **synchronize** all our clocks.
  (a.) compare   (b.) wind   (c.) take apart   (d.) match times on

21. Building a stone wall is a **laborious** task.
  (a.) difficult   (b.) long   (c.) simple   (d.) unionized

22. Cal's neighborhood is full of friendly and **upright** citizens.
  (a.) well-known   (b.) morally good   (c.) uncaring   (d.) concerned

23. The fans all **idolize** the team's quarterback.
  (a.) adore   (b.) mimic   (c.) fear   (d.) criticize

24. **Disposal** of toxic materials is an important environmental issue.
  (a.) manufacturing   (b.) using   (c.) discarding   (d.) collection

25. The senator's reaction to the scandal may **taint** his reputation.
  (a.) make fun of   (b.) describe   (c.) harm   (d.) praise

26. Our science teacher showed us how to create a **vacuum** in a container.
  (a.) vapor   (b.) empty space   (c.) model   (d.) experiment

27. Rescue workers rushed to the site of the **catastrophe**.
  (a.) festival   (b.) disaster   (c.) drill   (d.) convention

28. The racers ran to the pole, **pivoted** around it, and hopped back.
(a.) rotated   (b.) dug   (c.) danced   (d.) landscaped

29. Dad tried to **dilute** the old paint with turpentine.
(a.) mix   (b.) remove   (c.) apply   (d.) thin

30. The jurors felt that the doctor was a **credible** witness.
(a.) dramatic   (b.) unbelievable   (c.) reliable   (d.) medical

31. The scientists prepared for the **venture** in the rainforest.
(a.) risky task   (b.) village   (c.) camping trip   (d.) film crew

32. The quiz show contestant made a **haphazard** guess.
(a.) educated   (b.) chance   (c.) desperate   (d.) dangerous

33. Sara didn't realize that her **flippant** remark would hurt Sandy's feelings.
(a.) offhand   (b.) friendly   (c.) noisy   (d.) nasty

34. The principal asked for volunteers to make a **platform** for the exhibit.
(a.) advertisement   (b.) guidebook   (c.) raised floor   (d.) area

35. The **dimensions** of the crate are large enough for the statue.
(a.) contents   (b.) measurements   (c.) decorations   (d.) sides

36. We like the food in the new restaurant, but the service is **mediocre**.
(a.) magnificent   (b.) terrible   (c.) slow   (d.) ordinary

37. After marching all day, the exhausted **platoon** returned to the base.
(a.) animal   (b.) military group   (c.) commander   (d.) pirate

38. Fred woke up early to begin his **hectic** day.
(a.) very windy   (b.) ordinary   (c.) important   (d.) very hurried

39. Bill and Paula are sure they can **engineer** a robot in time for the science fair.
(a.) motorize   (b.) control   (c.) disassemble   (d.) build

40. After the meal, the waiter brought out a tray of **savory** desserts.
(a.) delicious   (b.) melting   (c.) bland   (d.) expensive

41. Dorothy bought a **diminutive** curtain for the dollhouse.
(a.) antique   (b.) torn   (c.) tiny   (d.) lacy

42. Anything that helps the environment is **beneficial** for everyone.
(a.) popular   (b.) dangerous   (c.) helpful   (d.) harmful

43. There must be a **plausible** explanation for the scary noise.
(a.) unbelievable   (b.) believable   (c.) lengthy   (d.) confused

44. The **perimeter** of the lake measures exactly three miles.
(a.) depth (b.) distance around (c.) distance across (d.) width

45. Even mountain climbers couldn't get up the **vertical** cliff.
(a.) rocky (b.) sloping (c.) extremely high (d.) straight up and down

46. We listened as the alleged felon tried to **hedge** the reporter's question.
(a.) answer (b.) avoid (c.) ask (d.) shout

47. The archaeologists found only a **vestige** of the ancient city.
(a.) trace (b.) map (c.) exploration (d.) legend

48. The engineers **devised** a plan to reroute traffic around the construction site.
(a.) demolished (b.) opened (c.) revealed (d.) invented

49. Grandpa spun a good **yarn** about his trip to Florida.
(a.) joke (b.) nature essay (c.) adventure story (d.) travelogue

50. No one has ever been able to discover the pirate's **plunder**.
(a.) secret (b.) name (c.) good news (d.) stolen goods

51. The baby penguin will **flourish** on the new diet.
(a.) chew (b.) thrive (c.) get sick (d.) become overweight

52. The **voluble** child wore out the babysitter.
(a.) active (b.) obedient (c.) talkative (d.) moody

53. When questioned by the police, the witness gave a **hesitant** answer.
(a.) undecided (b.) incorrect (c.) firm (d.) positive

54. The principal **commended** Alan's essay about the community.
(a.) disliked (b.) praised (c.) read aloud (d.) graded

55. Franco hoped for the opportunity to **portray** the detective.
(a.) act the part of (b.) call for (c.) hire (d.) deceive

56. Be firm but gentle when you **discipline** your new puppy.
(a.) chase (b.) feed (c.) punish (d.) spoil

57. The astronomer explained his **hypothesis** about asteroids.
(a.) book (b.) understanding (c.) telescope (d.) theory

58. The executives met to **transact** the business of joining the two companies.
(a.) put an end to (b.) encourage (c.) carry out (d.) witness

59. Grandma keeps a **hoard** of jelly beans for our visits.
a. stored supply   b. large amount   c. gift   d. locked cabinet

60. We all complained about the new manager's **dominant** personality.
a. largest   b. obedient   c. quietest   d. controlling

61. The **weary** traveler was glad when the long flight ended.
a. elderly   b. tired   c. experienced   d. excited

62. After moving to her new neighborhood, Kara felt **disconnected** from everyone.
a. sleepy   b. pensive   c. detached   d. negative

63. Mrs. Wells is my father's **colleague**.
a. partner   b. enemy   c. friend   d. boss

64. The new soldiers wondered if they would see the general's **wrath**.
a. rage   b. plan   c. flowers   d. grief

65. My brother was sent on a two-week **furlough**.
a. mission   b. convention   c. isolation   d. vacation

66. We planned to get an early start, but fate **intervened**.
a. interviewed   b. helped out   c. interfered   d. questioned

67. The scientist gave us a **precise** answer.
a. blurted   b. exact   c. incorrect   d. garbled

68. The stray kitten looked wet and **wretched**.
a. angry   b. feverish   c. striped   d. miserable

69. The rivalry between the teams caused **discord** between the two schools.
a. disagreement   b. hysteria   c. friendship   d. good behavior

70. The little mouse skillfully avoided the **predator**.
a. soldier   b. trap   c. hunter   d. automobile

71. Making a speech is an **ordeal** for Dan.
a. honor   b. trial   c. joy   d. experience

72. The **humble** firefighters declared that they were only doing their job.
a. quiet   b. brilliant   c. clumsy   d. modest

73. The drama coach held a **preliminary** meeting for everyone who wanted to try out for the play.
a. introductory   b. informal   c. long   d. scheduled

74. The flashbulb's bright light made the students **flinch**.
a. smile   b. wince   c. laugh   d. sob

5

75. The chimp's show of **hostility** is only a game.
   (a.) good manners   (b.) grief   (c.) unfriendliness   (d.) cheerfulness

76. Rachel's mother helped her **disentangle** the ribbon from her hair.
   (a.) examine   (b.) break   (c.) tie   (d.) free

77. Kevin tried to act **nonchalant** about winning the race.
   (a.) smug   (b.) excited   (c.) unhappy   (d.) casual

78. The **presumptuous** journalist asked personal questions.
   (a.) overconfident   (b.) accurate   (c.) curious   (d.) prompt

79. The volunteer's **zeal** for the project made her its best worker.
   (a.) liveliness   (b.) enthusiasm   (c.) assignment   (d.) donation

80. When Aladdin **burnished** the lamp, the genie appeared.
   (a.) destroyed   (b.) polished   (c.) lit   (d.) turned off

81. Allie felt that boots would be the most **pragmatic** choice.
   (a.) difficult   (b.) impractical   (c.) expensive   (d.) practical

82. The talented **diplomat** brought an end to the crisis.
   (a.) chef   (b.) graduate   (c.) ambassador   (d.) elected official

83. The book store is small, but it has a **diverse** selection of books.
   (a.) large   (b.) varied   (c.) strange   (d.) divided

84. Flo leaped over the last **hurdle** to win the race.
   (a.) barrier   (b.) player   (c.) puddle   (d.) shrub

85. Abraham Lincoln is remembered as a **paragon** of honesty.
   (a.) story about   (b.) ideal example   (c.) mockery   (d.) lacking

86. The doctor's prescription was only **legible** to the druggist.
   (a.) unreadable   (b.) legal   (c.) written   (d.) clear

87. Bill felt a slight **twinge** when he ran on his sprained ankle.
   (a.) fall   (b.) regret   (c.) pain   (d.) burn

88. The pony **faltered** in front of the stream.
   (a.) hesitated   (b.) jumped   (c.) trotted   (d.) drank

89. The actor's **retort** made the audience cheer.
   (a.) witty reply   (b.) training   (c.) final exit   (d.) sneer

90. Later on, Luke came to **lament** his hasty remark.
   (a.) laugh at   (b.) recall   (c.) regret   (d.) blame

CHAPTER 1

WORD LIST

Read each word using the pronunciation key.

abduct (ab dukt´)
aspiration (as pə rā´ shən)
burnish (bər´ nish)
curiosity (kyо͝or ē äs´ ə tē)
diagnosis (dī əg nō´ sis)
disharmony (dis här´ mə nē)
effect (ə fekt´)
excursion (ik skər´ zhən)
finicky (fin´ i kē)
gaunt (gônt)
hygiene (hī´ jēn)
intolerable (in täl´ ər ə bəl)
lithe (līŧh)
nibble (nib´ əl)
persist (pər sist´)
prevalent (prev´ ə lənt)
renounce (ri nouns´)
skeptical (skep´ ti kəl)
swelter (swel´ tər)
unintelligible (un in tel´ i jə bəl)

WORD STUDY

Suffixes

The suffixes *-ion*, *-ation*, and *-tion* mean "the act or condition of."

connection (kə nek´ shən) *(n.)* the condition of being connected
hibernation (hī bər nā´ shən) *(n.)* the act of hibernating
illumination (i lо͞o mə nā´ shən) *(n.)* the condition of being illuminated or lit
observation (ob sərv ā´ shən) *(n.)* the act of observing
rotation (rō tā´ shən) *(n.)* the act of rotating or turning around
satisfaction (sat is fak´ shən) *(n.)* the condition of being satisfied

Challenge Words

dogmatic (dôg ma´ tik)
feckless (fek´ lis)
ramification (ram ə fə kā´ shən)
rancid (ran´ sid)
stagnant (stag´ nənt)

WORDS IN CONTEXT

Read each sentence below to figure out the meaning of the word in **bold**. Use reasoning skills and the remainder of the sentence to help you. Write the meaning of the word on the line.

1. The family piled chairs, snacks, towels, and cameras into the car for an **excursion** to the beach.

   _____

2. With her political **aspirations** in mind, my sister applied for a job with our state senator.

   _____

3. Because of the drought, the ranchers had very little to feed their **gaunt** cattle.

   _____

4. The doctor ran several tests before she made a **diagnosis**.

   _____

5. Daisy **burnished** the car with a lint-free cloth.

   _____

6. Maggie and Molly continued to work in **disharmony** until they finally settled their argument.

   _____

7. We learned in health class that personal **hygiene** helps prevent the spread of germs.

   _____

8. After four hours of **intolerable** noise, the drilling finally stopped.

   _____

9. I'm not really hungry, but I would like a **nibble** of your cheesecake.

   _____

10. Jim took one last breath of cool air before going out to **swelter** in the heat.

   _____

WORD MEANINGS

Word Learning

Study the spelling, part(s) of speech, and meaning(s) of each word. Complete each sentence by writing the word on the line. Then read the sentence.

1. **abduct** *(v.)* to carry off by force

   The villains intend to _____ the millionaire's child.

2. **aspiration** *(n.)* a hope of achievement

   Since James's _____ is to become a musician, he practices the cello every day.

3. **burnish** *(v.)* 1. to polish by rubbing; 2. to make glossy and smooth

   My mother uses a special cream to _____ the silver.

4. **curiosity** *(n.)* a desire to learn or know about something

   My _____ got the better of me, and I read the end of the book first.

5. **diagnosis** *(n.)* 1. an act of identifying a certain illness; 2. a conclusion reached about something

   After the test, we waited eagerly for the doctor's _____.

6. **disharmony** *(n.)* 1. lack of agreement or harmony; 2. discord

   The barnyard animals mooed, honked, bleated, and crowed in

   _____.

7. **effect** *(n.)* 1. a result; 2. outcome caused by something; *(v.)* to bring about or cause to happen

   You do not understand the _____ of your actions.

   The president began to _____ changes in club procedures.

8. **excursion** *(n.)* 1. a short journey; 2. a pleasure trip

   Mr. Cruz wants to join our _____ to the Museum of Medicine.

9. **finicky** *(adj.)* 1. difficult to please; 2. very fussy; 3. fastidious

   My sister is such a _____ eater.

10. **gaunt** *(adj.)* 1. thin and bony; 2. angular

    Her wedding ring hung loosely on her _____ finger.

11. **hygiene** *(n.)* the science of personal health and disease prevention

    Be sure to practice good _____.

12. **intolerable** *(adj.)* 1. unbearable; 2. beyond what is acceptable

    Last summer we suffered _____ heat.

13. **lithe** *(adj.)* able to bend easily

    The _____ gymnasts did somersaults across the mat.

14. **nibble** *(v.)* to eat or chew in small, quick bites; *(n.)* a small bite

    Watch that mouse _____ at the peanut butter.

    I'll just have a _____ of your sandwich.

15. **persist** *(v.)* 1. to refuse to stop; 2. to continue firmly in an action or a thought

    If you _____ in playing your music, I'll have to make a formal complaint.

16. **prevalent** *(adj.)* widely or commonly found

    The belief in independence is _____ among Americans.

17. **renounce** *(v.)* 1. to give up a title, a responsibility, or an activity; 2. to reject

    Many people _____ their bad habits on New Year's Day.

18. **skeptical** *(adj.)* 1. doubting; 2. questioning; 3. not quickly or easily believing

    Kitty Jones claimed innocence, but the judge looked _____.

19. **swelter** *(v.)* to be affected by high heat

    We'll _____ all day in the hot sun.

20. **unintelligible** *(adj.)* not able to be understood

    Nothing but _____ noises came through the wall.

Notable Quotes

"Far away in the sunshine are my highest **aspirations**. I may not reach them, but I can look up and see their beauty, believe in them, and try to follow where they lead."

—Louisa May Alcott (1832–1888), novelist

Use Your Vocabulary

Choose the word from the Word List that best completes each sentence. Write the word on the line. You may use the plural form of nouns and the past tense of verbs if necessary.

When I heard that domesticated cats descended from the African wildcat, I was __1__, but then I read it in the encyclopedia. The information stirred my __2__, so I checked out several books about cats. Cheetahs were __3__ from their native habitats and were trained as hunting animals by royalty in the Middle East and India. The __4__ belief among experts is that today's Abyssinian cats probably look most like the cats that lived in ancient Egypt. The Sphynx cat is hairless and has large ears, so it looks __5__ even when healthy and well-fed. In 1851, the first cat show was held in England for people who had __6__ of greatness for their cats.

A cat has a(n) __7__ body that can twist and turn in amazing ways. It utters a variety of __8__ meows, hisses, yelps, and purrs, but a sensitive cat owner can tell the difference between expressions of hunger, anger, pain, and contentment. Also, a cat's owner may need to take a sick cat to see a veterinarian for a proper __9__ and medication. Many pets require grooming, but a cat looks after its own __10__ by licking its fur smooth and clean. A cat uses its long, rough tongue with the same __11__ as a hairbrush or a scrubbing brush. A cat does not have sweat glands, but it may pant when it begins to __12__ on a hot day. Cats have a coating at the back of their eyes. This coating reflects direct light like __13__ metal. A cat sets the boundaries of its territory and very rarely makes __14__ outside of that area. Several cats living in the same household may have their moments of __15__, but they usually learn to get along.

I have a very __16__ cat who eats only canned tuna. He eats only a few __17__ at a time. My mother finds it __18__ that he jumps onto the kitchen counter. "I will __19__ all responsibility for that cat if he does not stop!" she said. Fortunately, he has learned not to __20__.

1. _____
2. _____
3. _____
4. _____
5. _____
6. _____
7. _____
8. _____
9. _____
10. _____
11. _____
12. _____
13. _____
14. _____
15. _____
16. _____
17. _____
18. _____
19. _____
20. _____

SYNONYMS

Synonyms are words that have the same or nearly the same meanings.

Part 1 Choose the word from the box that is the best synonym for each group of words. Write the word on the line.

aspiration	excursion	gaunt	hygiene
intolerable	lithe	prevalent	unintelligible

1. prominent, widespread, accepted _____

2. cleanliness, sanitation, health _____

3. a tour, jaunt, expedition _____

4. skinny, emaciated, scrawny, haggard _____

5. unendurable, impossible _____

6. ambition, yearning, desire _____

7. flexible, supple, pliable _____

8. meaningless, incomprehensible _____

Part 2 Replace the underlined word with a word from the box that means the same or almost the same. Write your answer on the line.

persists	burnished	skeptical	diagnosis
swelter	abduct	renounce	

9. Uncle Jim offered his <u>analysis</u> of the situation by saying that we need more working space in the basement. _____

10. If the cold weather <u>lasts</u>, we will all go crazy. _____

11. I have no wish to <u>sweat</u> in this heat until dinnertime. _____

12. The silver locket was <u>polished</u> by the blowing desert sand. _____

13. O my Queen! I beg of you, do not <u>forsake</u> your only daughter!

_____

14. They tried to <u>kidnap</u> the senator but were caught. _____

15. The police remain <u>doubtful</u> about the thieves' intentions.

_____

 **ANTONYMS**

Antonyms are words that have opposite or nearly opposite meanings.

Part 1 Choose the word from the box that is the best antonym for each group of words. Write the word on the line.

> burnish   disharmony   finicky   intolerable   skeptical

1. pleasing, satisfying, bearable _____

2. agreement, pleasant sounds _____

3. convinced, accepting, sure _____

4. not hard to please, easygoing _____

5. dull, dim _____

Part 2 Replace the underlined word with a word from the box that means the opposite or almost the opposite. Write your answer on the line.

> unintelligible   renounce   gaunt   prevalent   lithe

6. Mrs. Lang stretched out her hands and looked at her <u>stiff</u> fingers.

_____

7. In the dry grass, we saw a <u>stout</u> rabbit. _____

8. Such ideas are <u>rare</u> in this part of the country. _____

9. Ebenezer is unlikely to <u>keep</u> his vow. _____

10. The cashier said something <u>meaningful</u>. _____

WORD STUDY

Suffixes Choose the word from the box that best completes each sentence.

connection	hibernation	illumination
observation	rotation	satisfaction

1. Carey toasted the marshmallows to his _____.

2. Woe to the hiker who disturbs the bear's winter _____.

3. After close _____, I grew to understand the ape's behavior.

4. Alex grew dizzy from watching the _____ of the merry-go-round.

5. What is your _____ with the family?

6. The _____ of the street lamps casts an eerie glow.

Vocabulary in Action

The words *effect* and *affect* are easy to confuse with each other. Even journalists and English teachers sometimes have to stop and think about whether their sentence calls for *effect* or *affect*.

The word *effect* is almost always a noun, while *affect* is almost always a verb. So you may find it helpful to determine whether the sentence needs a verb or a noun.

Examples of *affect*, a verb: We were deeply affected by the film. The weather affects our moods. The quality of your work affects your grades.

Examples of *effect*, a noun: The effect of the new rule on the children was profound. The effect of diligent study habits is better learning.

Here are three easy tips to help you determine which is the correct word in a sentence.

Tip 1: Determine whether the usage calls for a noun or a verb.

Tip 2: If a verb is needed, you will almost always choose "affect," which means "to change or alter."

Tip 3: When a noun is needed, you will almost always choose "effect," which means "a result."

CHALLENGE WORDS

Word Learning—Challenge!

Study the spelling, part of speech, and meaning(s) of each word. Complete each sentence by writing the word on the line. Then read the sentence.

1. **dogmatic** *(adj.)* 1. opinionated; 2. arrogant

   Her _____ approach to the issue made it impossible to argue with her.

2. **feckless** *(adj.)* 1. ineffective; 2. irresponsible; 3. careless

   I hope you will not be influenced by Tom's _____ behavior.

3. **ramification** *(n.)* 1. the result or outcome of an act; 2. a consequence

   Whoever pulled that prank obviously did not realize its _____; we were cleaning up for hours.

4. **rancid** *(adj.)* 1. having an awful odor or taste; 2. offensive

   After being in the car all day, the meat had turned _____.

5. **stagnant** *(adj.)* 1. stale; 2. not advancing or developing

   You won't catch any fish in that _____ pond.

Use Your Vocabulary—Challenge!

The Search Begins Checkerboard, your pet cat, has gotten out of the house and you haven't seen her in several days. You are worried that she can't take care of herself in the wild woods near your home. Using the Challenge Words above, write a story about your search for Checkerboard on a separate piece of paper. Be sure to include a beginning, a middle, and an end. Use your imagination to make the story interesting.

> ### Notable Quotes
>
> "Iron rusts from disuse; **stagnant** water loses its purity and in cold weather becomes frozen; even so does inaction sap the vigor of the mind."
>
> —Leonardo da Vinci (1452–1519), Italian inventor, artist, mathematician (from *The Notebooks*)

FUN WITH WORDS

Use the clues to complete the puzzle. Choose from the vocabulary words in this chapter.

Across

4. You have this when you set a goal.

6. This "killed" the cat that wanted to know too much.

7. You do this if you want something badly enough.

10. After you get one, you might want a second opinion.

11. Mice do this to cheese.

12. A ruler in trouble might _____ his throne or office.

13. A cause always has one.

Down

1. Always be _____ of a deal that sounds too good to be true.

2. Speech sounds like this on a bad phone connection.

3. If something is dull, you do this to it.

4. A radio broadcast in 1938 made people believe Martians were going to _____ them.

5. People who are this about food may cook for themselves.

7. A(n) _____ opinion is one held by many people.

8. You need this kind of body to compete as an Olympic diver.

9. You'll start to do this if you stay in the sun too long.

CHAPTER 2

WORD LIST

Read each word using the pronunciation key.

absurd (əb sərd´)
astound (ə stound´)
calamity (kə lam´ ə tē)
decelerate (dē sel´ ə rāt)
dialect (dī´ ə lekt)
dishonor (dis on´ ər)
efficient (i fish´ ənt)
exert (ig zərt´)
finite (fī´ nīt)
glutton (glut´ ən)
hypothesis (hī päth´ ə sis)
inundate (in´ ən dāt)
luminous (lōō´ mə nəs)
niche (nich)
persuasive (pər swā´ siv)
prohibit (prō hib´ it)
retort (ri tôrt´)
snare (snâr)
synchronize (sīŋ´ krə niz)
upheaval (up hē´ vəl)

WORD STUDY

Analogies

Analogies show relationships between pairs of words. Study the relationships between the pairs of words in the analogies below.

chick is to **hen** as **kitten** is to **cat**

napkin is to **lap** as **tablecloth** is to **table**

cage is to **parakeet** as **aquarium** is to **fish**

Challenge Words

admonish (ad mon´ ish)
exacerbate (ig zas´ ər bāt)
expedient (ek spē´ dē ənt)
superfluous (sōō pər´ flōō əs)
versatile (vər´ sə təl)

WORDS IN CONTEXT

Read each sentence below to figure out the meaning of the word in **bold**. Use reasoning skills and the remainder of the sentence to help you. Write the meaning of the word on the line.

1. Although we had prepared for the hurricane, the effects of the **calamity** overwhelmed us.

   _____

2. When Nikki shouted a question from the audience, the comedian responded with a clever **retort**.

   _____

3. With our grandfather's fishing net, Mark set a **snare** for the next person to walk through the door.

   _____

4. I **astounded** my friends with my new magic tricks.

   _____

5. I made a **glutton** of myself at Thanksgiving dinner, and I paid for it in stomach pains.

   _____

6. There is no **dishonor** in losing if you have performed well.

   _____

7. To calm my anger, I lifted my eyes to the **luminous**, starry sky.

   _____

8. **Dialects** vary from region to region, and people in the South speak differently from people in the North.

   _____

9. Your ideas are **absurd**; I don't even want to hear them.

   _____

10. If we **synchronize** our schedules, we'll be able to eat lunch together.

    _____

WORD MEANINGS

Word Learning

Study the spelling, part(s) of speech, and meaning(s) of each word. Complete each sentence by writing the word on the line. Then read the sentence.

1. **absurd** *(adj.)* 1. ridiculous or unreasonable; 2. not true

   Please don't give me such _____ requests on short notice.

2. **astound** *(v.)* 1. to fill with wonder; 2. to surprise

   Her marvelous talents continue to _____ me.

3. **calamity** *(n.)* 1. a disaster; 2. great distress or misfortune

   We managed to avoid a _____ by putting out the fire right away.

4. **decelerate** *(v.)* to decrease the speed of

   Remember to _____ the car before pulling into the driveway.

5. **dialect** *(n.)* a variation of pronunciation, grammar, or vocabulary by a group within a language or region

   That man's _____ is particular to a region in Mexico.

6. **dishonor** *(n.)* 1. loss of one's good name; 2. shame; *(v.)* 1. to deprive of one's good name; 2. to shame; 3. to disgrace

   The traitor's behavior was a great _____ to her country.

   Do not _____ my family by speaking to me that way!

7. **efficient** *(adj.)* operating well, without wasted time, energy, or material

   I see you've developed a very _____ system of making shoes.

8. **exert** *(v.)* 1. to put into action; 2. to exercise or use

   Daniel had to _____ all of his strength to reach the top of the tree.

9. **finite** *(adj.)* 1. having an end; 2. having bounds or limits; 3. measurable

   The Earth has _____ reserves of oil.

10. **glutton** *(n.)* a person or an animal that eats too much

    "The _____ didn't leave any spinach for me!" she said laughingly.

11. **hypothesis** *(n.)* an unproved theory, statement, or guess that is based on facts

    I'd like to test that _____.

12. **inundate** *(v.)* 1. to overwhelm; 2. to overflow

The prize giveaway caused listeners to _____ the radio station with phone calls.

13. **luminous** *(adj.)* 1. giving light; 2. full of light; 3. bright

A _____ candle burned in the window.

14. **niche** *(n.)* 1. a hollow space within a wall, rock, or hill; 2. a place or position well-suited to the person in it

Marietta found her _____ playing the triangle in the school orchestra.

15. **persuasive** *(adj.)* having the ability to convince

She made a very _____ argument for donating the money.

16. **prohibit** *(v.)* to forbid an action by rule or law

The managers decided to _____ smoking in the restaurant.

17. **retort** *(v.)* 1. to answer quickly; 2. to reply with a prompt argument; *(n.)* a fast or witty response

After the accusation, the judge will expect you to _____.

My sister always has a quick _____ for any remark.

18. **snare** *(n.)* 1. a trap, usually with a noose, for catching animals; 2. any trap; *(v.)* to trap

The rangers set a _____ in the forest.

The villain prepared to _____ her victim.

19. **synchronize** *(v.)* 1. to make agree in time; 2. to match the rate of movement of two things

It's time to _____ our watches.

20. **upheaval** *(n.)* 1. the act of being thrown upward; 2. an uprising or a violent upset

The earthquake created a huge _____ of land.

Notable Quotes

"In the highest civilization, the book is still the highest delight. He who has once known its satisfactions is provided with a resource against **calamity**."

—Ralph Waldo Emerson (1803–1882), poet, philosopher (from *Letters and Social Aims: Quotation and Originality*)

Use Your Vocabulary

Choose the word from the Word List that best completes each sentence. Write the word on the line. You may use the plural form of nouns and the past tense of verbs if necessary.

I was in the yard at my grandparents farm when the __1__ struck. The sky had an eerie, __2__ quality, although the clouds were quite dark. My grandparents listened to the tornado warnings on the radio. The radio announcer spoke with a heavy __3__ that I couldn't understand. It had been raining all day. The fields and garden were __4__ with water, but now the rain had stopped. The wind had __5__ too. Everything was calm and still. Suddenly, my grandparents came out of the house, walking quickly with almost __6__ steps. Grandma was carrying Larry, her plump, hefty cat.

"Head for the storm cellar," Grandpa said. "The tornado is headed right for us, and we have only a(n) __7__ amount of time to get ready."

"I don't see any funnel cloud," I said. "Maybe the weather forecaster's __8__ is wrong."

"Do you want to wait up here and find out?" Grandpa __9__. I looked again at the dark, swirling clouds and realized I was being __10__. There was no __11__ in being prepared for the worst.

We headed for the storm cellar. Since Grandpa keeps the doors well-oiled, he did not have to __12__ much effort to open them. Grandma keeps the cellar supplied and organized in a very __13__ manner.

"I knew our furry, little __14__ wouldn't be happy without his food," Grandma said with a grin. Larry jumped from Grandma's arms and settled into a(n) __15__ at the back of the cellar.

Without warning, the roar of the tornado filled the cellar and __16__ conversation. I was __17__ by the way the locked doors shook and rattled. Even Grandpa's hunting __18__, hanging under the stairs, swayed back and forth.

We were lucky. The __19__ of several big trees on the property only damaged some fences. Seeing the areas directly hit by the tornado was a(n) __20__ lesson. I'll take tornado warnings seriously from now on.

1. _____
2. _____
3. _____
4. _____
5. _____
6. _____
7. _____
8. _____
9. _____
10. _____
11. _____
12. _____
13. _____
14. _____
15. _____
16. _____
17. _____
18. _____
19. _____
20. _____

SYNONYMS

Synonyms are words that have the same or nearly the same meanings.

Part 1 Choose the word from the box that is the best synonym for each group of words. Write the word on the line.

astound	decelerate	finite	hypothesis
persuasive	retort	snare	upheaval

1. eruption, agitation, unrest _____

2. effective, convincing, influential _____

3. opinion, theory, supposition _____

4. respond; quick answer _____

5. restricted, limited, bounded _____

6. slow down _____

7. amaze, shock, bewilder _____

8. net, lure; entangle _____

Part 2 Replace the underlined word with a word from the box that means the same or almost the same. Write your answer on the line.

luminous	inundated	exert	calamity
niche	absurd	prohibit	

9. The new laws will <u>prevent</u> parking on the streets at night. _____

10. The baby bird sat tucked in a <u>cranny</u> in the wall. _____

11. From miles away, we could see the <u>glowing</u> city lights. _____

12. The catalog was <u>flooded</u> with orders for new computers. _____

13. After his surgery, my father was not allowed to <u>strain</u> himself.

   _____

14. It took the family months to recover from the <u>disaster</u>. _____

15. Who would be so <u>foolish</u> as to eat peas with a knife? _____

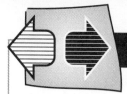

ANTONYMS

Antonyms are words that have opposite or nearly opposite meanings.

Part 1 Choose the word from the box that is the best antonym for each group of words. Write the word on the line.

| decelerate | absurd | persuasive | snare | hypothesis |

1. rational, reasonable, logical _____

2. speed up, accelerate _____

3. free, let go, liberate _____

4. proven fact _____

5. discouraging, deterring _____

Part 2 Replace the underlined word with a word from the box that means the opposite or almost the opposite. Write your answer on the line.

| prohibit | upheaval | luminous | efficient | finite |

6. The winter was a time of great <u>stillness</u> in our house. _____

7. The children had a <u>limitless</u> supply of toys. _____

8. Our heating system is very <u>wasteful</u>. _____

9. Every house on the block had <u>dark</u> windows. _____

10. Our neighbors did not want to <u>permit</u> snowball throwing in the street.

_____

Vocabulary in Action

The word **luminous** ("full of light") first appeared around 1432 and comes from the Latin word *luminosus*, which means "shining, full of light." Other words with the same Latin root include *translucent* and *illuminate*.

Analogies To complete the following analogies, decide what kind of relationship is shown by the first pair of words. Then fill in the bubble next to the pair of words that show the same relationship.

1. **hinder** is to **help** as
   - (a.) spray is to dig
   - (b.) forbid is to permit
   - (c.) think is to consider
   - (d.) scrape is to cut

2. **irritate** is to **mosquito** as
   - (a.) climb is to bumblebee
   - (b.) befriend is to spider
   - (c.) entertain is to comedian
   - (d.) sell is to lawyer

3. **scamper** is to **squirrel** as
   - (a.) glide is to airplane
   - (b.) rest is to nest
   - (c.) joke is to clown
   - (d.) eat is to chipmunk

4. **native** is to **foreign** as
   - (a.) friendly is to talkative
   - (b.) funny is to laughable
   - (c.) adventurous is to wonderful
   - (d.) familiar is to unknown

5. **compose** is to **poem** as
   - (a.) study is to library
   - (b.) write is to idea
   - (c.) construct is to house
   - (d.) earn is to bank

6. **depart** is to **farewell** as
   - (a.) arrive is to greeting
   - (b.) forget is to congratulation
   - (c.) sail is to departure
   - (d.) arrive is to expectation

Vocabulary in Action

To better understand analogies, rephrase the analogy in words that explain the relationships between the objects in the analogy. For example, in the analogy "chick is to hen as kitten is to cat," you might write "This analogy gives examples of baby animals and their adult counterparts." For the analogy "napkin is to lap as tablecloth is to table," you might say "The first items in each series cover and protect the second items in the analogy." How might you rephrase or describe the third analogy in the Word Study?

CHALLENGE WORDS

Word Learning—Challenge!

Study the spelling, part of speech, and meaning(s) of each word. Complete each sentence by writing the word on the line. Then read the sentence.

1. **admonish** *(v.)* to criticize or scold someone in a mild way

   Melissa _____ her younger brother for teasing the chipmunk.

2. **exacerbate** *(v.)* 1. to make something worse than it is; 2. to aggravate

   If you also come late you will only _____ the situation.

3. **expedient** *(adj.)* 1. useful for creating a desired result; 2. based on self-interest

   It would be most _____ to park the car right in front.

4. **superfluous** *(adj.)* in excess of what is called for or necessary

   I have no need for this _____ chatter.

5. **versatile** *(adj.)* 1. able to do a number of things right; 2. useful for many functions

   I am looking for a _____ jacket for both winter and spring.

Use Your Vocabulary—Challenge!

Project Protect After a tornado hit their town, all of the town's schools decide to build tornado shelters. They don't want to be caught unprepared by the next tornado. Jackie and Sam are in charge of organizing the shelter for their school, but they don't always get along with each other. Using the Challenge Words above, write a story about their project. Explain the problems they face and the solutions they reach.

> *Notable Quotes*
>
> "Animation can explain whatever the mind of man can conceive. This facility makes it the most **versatile** and explicit means of communication yet devised for quick mass appreciation."
>
> —Walt Disney (1901–1966), film producer and pioneer of animated cartoon films

FUN WITH WORDS

Create a word search using 10 vocabulary words from the Basic Words list. Trade with a friend. Who can finish the word search first?

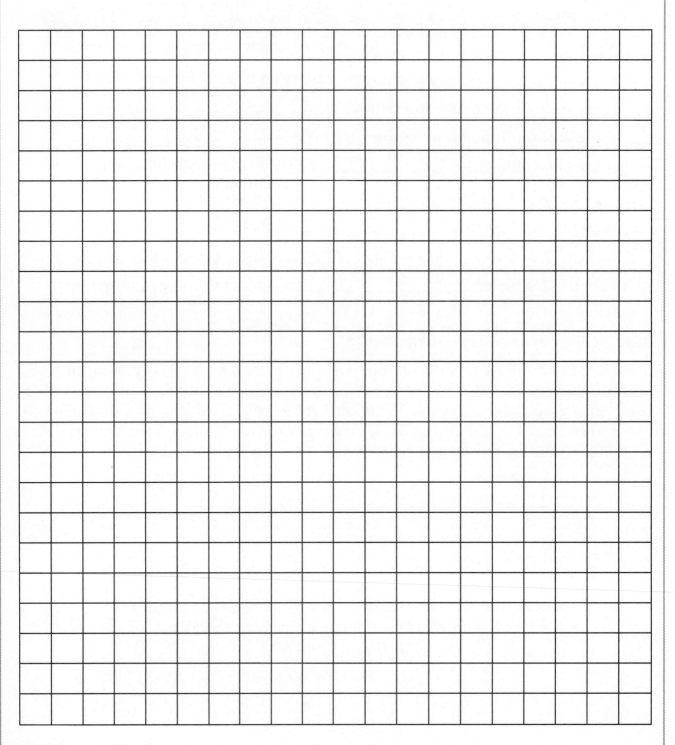

CHAPTER 3

WORD LIST

Read each word using the pronunciation key.

accessory (ak ses´ ə rē)
avenge (ə venj´)
catastrophe (kə tas´ trə fē)
decompose (dē kəm pōz´)
dilapidated (di lap´ ə dāt id)
dismay (dis mā´)
elapse (i laps´)
exhaust (ig zôst´)
flinch (flinch)
gorge (gôrj)
hysteria (his târ´ ē ə)
irascible (i ras´ ə bəl)
lyrics (lēr´ iks)
nominee (näm ə nē´)
petition (pə tish´ ən)
quirk (kwərk)
ruckus (ruk´ əs)
sopping (säp´ piŋ)
taint (tānt)
upkeep (up´ kēp)

WORD STUDY

Root Words

The Latin root *ag* or *act* means "to do" or "to drive."

action (ak´ shən) *(n.)* the state of doing something
active (ak´ tiv) *(n.)* tending to action; busy
agenda (ə jen´ də) *(n.)* a list of things to be done
agent (ā´ jənt) *(n.)* someone who does something
agile (aj´ əl) *(adj.)* able to do or move easily and quickly
enact (en akt´) *(v.)* to cause to be done

Challenge Words

anomaly (ə näm´ ə lē)
lucid (lōō´ sid)
misconstrue (mis cun strōō´)
mundane (mun dān´)
reprieve (ri prēv´)

WORDS IN CONTEXT

Read each sentence below to figure out the meaning of the word in **bold**. Use reasoning skills and the remainder of the sentence to help you. Write the meaning of the word on the line.

1. I don't understand the meaning of the **lyrics** to that song.

   _____

2. Each political party will choose a presidential **nominee** at its convention.

   _____

3. Spring rains on the plateau caused flash flooding in the **gorge**.

   _____

4. Please stop that **ruckus**, or you'll wake the baby!

   _____

5. We felt **dismay** after seeing all the litter at the campsite.

   _____

6. The countess planned to **avenge** the wrongs done to her father.

   _____

7. I have been in charge of the **upkeep** of my room since I was six years old.

   _____

8. The roof of that **dilapidated** old cottage is about to cave in.

   _____

9. An hour **elapsed** while we waited for Ramona to come home.

   _____

10. My stepfather thinks that if I tell too many jokes in class, it will **taint** my reputation as a serious student.

    _____

WORD MEANINGS

Word Learning

Study the spelling, part(s) of speech, and meaning(s) of each word. Complete each sentence by writing the word on the line. Then read the sentence.

1. **accessory** *(n.)* 1. an extra element or feature; 2. one who helps in a crime

   My cousin said the sun roof was an _____ she definitely wanted on her car.

2. **avenge** *(v.)* 1. to return some wrongdoing; 2. to take revenge

   Callie swore she would _____ the hurtful insult.

3. **catastrophe** *(n.)* a great, sudden disaster

   The accident proved to be a life-threatening _____.

4. **decompose** *(v.)* 1. to break down into parts; 2. to decay

   Dead plants and animals eventually _____ on the forest floor.

5. **dilapidated** *(adj.)* 1. in a state of ruin or disrepair; 2. falling to pieces

   He kept his paintings in a _____ barn.

6. **dismay** *(v.)* 1. to fill with fear; 2. to discourage or trouble; *(n.)* 1. fear at danger or trouble; 2. troubled state of mind

   Don't let my snake _____ you; it doesn't bite.

   Suong cast a look of _____ at the unkempt garden.

7. **elapse** *(v.)* 1. to pass by; 2. to slip away, usually with regard to time

   Time will _____ slowly when you have nothing to do.

8. **exhaust** *(v.)* 1. to use up; 2. to drain; 3. to let out air or fumes; *(n.)* fumes or gases from an engine

   If we keep eating, we will _____ our supply of snacks.

   The bus let out a thick black _____.

9. **flinch** *(v.)* 1. to show pain, fear, or surprise with a sudden movement; 2. to draw away

   I saw him _____ as the door slammed.

10. **gorge** *(n.)* a deep, narrow passage with steep, rocky walls; *(v.)* to stuff with something

    Our donkeys could not cross the _____.

    Don't _____ yourself with Halloween candy.

11. **hysteria** *(n.)* uncontrollable fear or emotion

    The appearance of the flying saucer led to mass _____.

12. **irascible** *(adj.)* 1. quick to anger; 2. hot-tempered

    I had heard about the _____ toddler, but I was not prepared for her tantrums.

13. **lyrics** *(n.)* the words of a song

    I like that melody, but I don't care for the _____.

14. **nominee** *(n.)* 1. a person who is nominated; 2. a person who is chosen as a political candidate

    The judges decided which _____ would win the grand prize.

15. **petition** *(n.)* 1. a written request for a certain action; 2. a strong request; *(v.)* 1. to make a request; 2. to seek

    We will circulate a _____ to build a new school.

    The neighborhood committee will _____ the city council for better garbage removal.

16. **quirk** *(n.)* 1. an odd behavior or mannerism; 2. accident

    Through some _____, Toni never paid for her ticket.

17. **ruckus** *(n.)* 1. a noisy commotion or disturbance; 2. an uproar

    Those construction workers cause such a _____!

18. **sopping** *(adj.)* soaking wet or drenched

    I came in from the rain with _____ shoes.

19. **taint** *(n.)* 1. to stain the honor of; 2. to dirty

    This mistake will certainly _____ his name as a good carpenter.

20. **upkeep** *(n.)* the act of keeping something in proper condition

    My teacher has charged me with the _____ of the reading corner.

Use Your Vocabulary

Choose the word from the Word List that best completes each sentence. Write the word on the line. You may use the plural form of nouns and the past tense of verbs if necessary.

On October 8, 1871, __1__ struck the city of Chicago. The Great Chicago Fire killed hundreds of people and left thousands homeless. Chicago has no hills, mountains, or __2__ to stop the wind from spreading a fire. The firefighters did their best, but to their __3__, the blaze grew out of control in less than two hours. They __4__ as the flames jumped across the Chicago River and engulfed the downtown area. Some areas of the city were filled with __5__ wooden shacks; the fire roared through these areas and continued to grow.

__6__ swept through the city. People filled the streets. Hundreds waded into Lake Michigan to escape the blaze, hoping that their __7__ clothes would protect them. Before long, the fire had __8__ the fire department and most of its water supplies. Days __9__ before the fire was brought under control.

Some people believed that an arsonist and his __10__ started the fire, but no one was ever charged with the crime. According to another story, a(n) __11__ in Mrs. O'Leary's barn started the fire. The __12__ of a song about the fire claim that Mrs. O'Leary's cow started it by kicking over a lantern. Some __13__ citizens wanted to __14__ the damage by punishing the O'Learys. Eventually, it was decided that no one had set the fire on purpose; it had happened through some horrible __15__ of fate.

Even though much of the city had been destroyed, the citizens did not allow it to __16__. They did not want the losses from the fire to __17__ their reputation as a growing, bustling city. They began immediately to rebuild. The city government heard a(n) __18__ for a change in the construction of houses. Elected officials and __19__ helped pass a construction code that required new buildings in Chicago to be made of brick. To this day, the __20__ of buildings in Chicago requires strict adherence to the city's fire code.

1. _____

2. _____

3. _____

4. _____

5. _____

6. _____

7. _____

8. _____

9. _____

10. _____

11. _____

12. _____

13. _____

14. _____

15. _____

16. _____

17. _____

18. _____

19. _____

20. _____

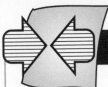

SYNONYMS

Synonyms are words that have the same or nearly the same meanings.

Part 1 Choose the word from the box that is the best synonym for each group of words. Write the word on the line.

hysteria	upkeep	quirk	dilapidated
catastrophe	sopping	petition	ruckus

1. maintenance, repair, preservation _____

2. soaked, dripping, saturated _____

3. appeal, plea; ask, beg _____

4. stir, fuss, hubbub _____

5. consuming fear, panic, excitement _____

6. irregularity, peculiarity, accident _____

7. run-down, neglected _____

8. a calamity, upheaval, destruction _____

Part 2 Replace the underlined word(s) with a word from the box that means the same or almost the same. Write your answer on the line.

decompose	avenge	taint	gorge
flinch	irascible	elapse	

9. My <u>crabby</u> neighbor does not like us to play ball in the yard.

   _____

10. How much time will <u>pass</u> before the situation changes? _____

11. The garbage in the yard will soon <u>rot</u>. _____

12. I'm afraid those chemicals will <u>pollute</u> our drinking water. _____

13. Let's <u>stuff</u> the sack with toys and candy. _____

14. She didn't even <u>wince</u> when the glass crashed to the floor. _____

15. He plotted to <u>get revenge</u> for the attack on his brother. _____

ANTONYMS

Antonyms are words that have opposite or nearly opposite meanings.

Part 1 Choose the word from the box that is the best antonym for each group of words. Write the word on the line.

decompose	**dilapidated**	**gorge**
irascible	**sopping**	**taint**

1. dry, dehydrated, arid _____

2. calm, agreeable, gracious _____

3. renewed, rebuilt, refinished _____

4. empty; a mountain peak _____

5. purify, cleanse _____

6. grow, improve _____

Part 2 Replace the underlined word with a word from the box that means the opposite or almost the opposite. Write your answer on the line.

hysteria	**avenge**	**petition**	**exhaust**	**dismayed**

7. I will not <u>forgive</u> that betrayal. _____

8. Don't <u>fill</u> our reserve of supplies for later. _____

9. She was <u>reassured</u> by the condition of her house after the storm.

_____

10. Please submit a written <u>command</u> to the school board. _____

11. I was overcome with <u>calmness</u>. _____

WORD STUDY

Root Words Choose the word from the box that best completes each of the following sentences.

> action   active   agenda
>
> agent   agile   enact

1. Have you written the _____ for this week's meeting?

2. Before I leave, I have to talk with my travel _____.

3. When are you going to clean your room? I'd like to see some

    _____.

4. That girl has an _____ membership in the outdoors club.

5. The village wants to _____ a law requiring everyone to recycle their trash.

6. My cat can't jump up on the counter anymore because she's not as

    _____ as she used to be.

Vocabulary in Action

It can be useful to study carefully a word's parts as a way of gaining a deeper understanding of the word. This is sometimes called parsing a word. When you parse a word, you give a grammatical description of the word and how it works in a sentence, or a part of speech. Using a good dictionary, see if you can parse some of the words below. Keep an eye out for surprising discoveries along the way!

Activism

Actionable

Agency

Agriculture

CHALLENGE WORDS

Word Learning—Challenge!

Study the spelling, part of speech, and meaning(s) of each word. Complete each sentence by writing the word on the line. Then read the sentence.

1. **anomaly** *(n.)* 1. something that is hard to classify; 2. something different

   Mei's exuberant nature makes her an _____ in her quiet family.

2. **lucid** *(adj.)* 1. having full understanding; 2. clear

   Although Mrs. Cruz is 95 years old, she is still quite _____.

3. **misconstrue** *(adj.)* 1. to think of in an incorrect way; 2. to misunderstand

   Don't _____ his silence as anger.

4. **mundane** *(adj.)* everyday, ordinary, or commonplace

   The squirrel is a fairly _____ example of a wild animal.

5. **reprieve** *(v.)* to delay or temporarily relieve

   Robin Hood asked the king to _____ his jail sentence.

Use Your Vocabulary—Challenge!

Diary Memories Mrs. O'Leary has left behind a diary with entries that describe her experiences during and after the Great Chicago Fire. Think about what you already know about Mrs. O'Leary. Imagine the experiences she might have had. Using the Challenge Words above, write a fictional diary entry. Use your imagination!

Vocabulary in Action

The word **mundane** comes from the Latin word *mundanus*, which means "belonging to the world." *Mundane* was originally designated as a way of distinguishing between that which was of the Church and that which was not of the Church. *Mundane* meant "worldly," "ordinary," or even "vulgar," as opposed to heavenly. Some synonyms for *mundane* include *dull, uninteresting, routine, everyday, commonplace, boring,* and *humdrum.*

FUN WITH WORDS

How closely did you read the story on page 35? Fill in the appropriate vocabulary word next to each clue. Then unscramble the circled letters to tell one theory about where the Great Chicago Fire started. Reread the story if you need help.

1. the words of a song
　　__ ◯ __ __ __ __

2. easily angered
　◯ __ __ __ __ ◯ __

3. a political appointee
　　◯ __ __ __ ◯ __

4. to trouble or scare
　　__ __ __ __ ◯ __

5. to draw back suddenly
　　__ ◯ __ __ __ __

6. a calamity
　__ ◯ __ __ ◯ __ __ __ __

7. to stain
　　__ ◯ __ __

8. dripping wet
　　__ ◯ __ __ __ ◯ __

9. a ravine
　　__ __ ◯ __ ◯

10. car fumes
　　__ __ ◯ __ __ ◯ __

Answer:

__ __ __ __ __ __ , __ __ __ __ __ __ __ , __

__ __ __ __

Review 1-3

Word Meanings Fill in the bubble next to the word that is best defined by each phrase.

1. to steal away
   - a. persist
   - b. abduct
   - c. astound
   - d. exert

2. a person who eats more than is healthy
   - a. glutton
   - b. nominee
   - c. curiosity
   - d. dialect

3. wringing wet
   - a. skeptical
   - b. prevalent
   - c. burnish
   - d. sopping

4. easily provoked or angered
   - a. finicky
   - b. irascible
   - c. intolerable
   - d. persuasive

5. to slow down
   - a. abduct
   - b. taint
   - c. inundate
   - d. decelerate

6. a state of disagreement
   - a. diagnosis
   - b. disharmony
   - c. dishonor
   - d. dismay

7. disease prevention through good health
   - a. petition
   - b. hypothesis
   - c. upheaval
   - d. hygiene

8. to be uncomfortably hot
   - a. decelerate
   - b. prohibit
   - c. swelter
   - d. exhaust

9. to get even for a wrongdoing
   - a. avenge
   - b. retort
   - c. snare
   - d. elapse

10. a terrible disaster
    - a. calamity
    - b. hygiene
    - c. swelter
    - d. aspiration

11. glowing or illuminated
    - a. gaunt
    - b. finite
    - c. luminous
    - d. irascible

12. to move at the same time or speed
    - a. synchronize
    - b. flinch
    - c. avenge
    - d. decompose

13. foolish or irrational
    - a. dilapidated
    - b. finicky
    - c. absurd
    - d. skeptical

14. to fill with fear
    - a. flinch
    - b. renounce
    - c. gorge
    - d. dismay

15. to refuse to give up
    - a. persist
    - b. exert
    - c. prohibit
    - d. elapse

16. getting results without wasting time or effort
    - a. unintelligible
    - b. luminous
    - c. sopping
    - d. efficient

17. to surrender something
    (a.)renounce   (b.)synchronize   (c.)dishonor   (d.)nibble

18. a request for action
    (a.)excursion   (b.)petition   (c.)calamity   (d.)catastrophe

19. the words of a song
    (a.)niche   (b.)exhaust   (c.)lyrics   (d.)dialect

20. cannot be understood
    (a.)intolerable   (b.)dilapidated   (c.)unintelligible   (d.)lithe

Sentence Completion Choose the word from the box that best completes each of the following sentences. Write the word in the blank.

accessories	nibble	effect	quirks	upkeep
burnishes	hysteria	niche	upheavals	ruckus

1. The American Revolution is one of the most famous political

   _____ in our history.

2. We calmed Mai's _____ by assuring her that her leg was not broken.

3. The _____ of the yard is my responsibility this summer.

4. Eating sugary foods can have a bad _____ on your teeth.

5. Reflectors and a light are important _____ for any bike.

6. Lynn found her _____ on the swimming team.

7. Once a year, Tom _____ his first-place tennis trophy.

8. A _____ erupted in the stands when our team won the championship.

9. "We all have our _____," Kirk said as he carefully folded and saved his gum wrapper.

10. I like to _____ on popcorn while I do my homework.

Fill in the Blanks

Fill in the bubble of the pair of words that best completes each sentence.

1. I was _____ about whether they could _____ such difficult moves in two short days.
   - (a.) skeptical, synchronize
   - (b.) finicky, avenge
   - (c.) persuasive, renounce
   - (d.) irascible, burnish

2. After the _____, the Earthquake Emergency Center was _____ by a flood of victims.
   - (a.) hysteria, dilapidated
   - (b.) catastrophe, inundated
   - (c.) diagnosis, prohibited
   - (d.) hypothesis, exhausted

3. The food was _____, even for a(n) _____ like me!
   - (a.) gaunt, ruckus
   - (b.) sopping, calamity
   - (c.) intolerable, glutton
   - (d.) absurd, excursion

4. _____ study habits will help you avoid a(n) _____ on next week's test.
   - (a.) Luminous, excursion
   - (b.) Unintelligible, upheaval
   - (c.) Efficient, calamity
   - (d.) Sopping, dialect

5. When Jamie is trying to _____ his influence, he can be very _____.
   - (a.) renounce, irascible
   - (b.) synchronize, unintelligible
   - (c.) exhaust, prevalent
   - (d.) exert, persuasive

6. The principal _____ activities that could cause _____ for our school.
   - (a.) decelerates, dismay
   - (b.) persists, retorts
   - (c.) prohibits, dishonor
   - (d.) avenges, curiosity

7. My younger sister raised a(n) _____ about buying the latest trendy _____.
   - (a.) ruckus, accessory
   - (b.) hysteria, upheaval
   - (c.) aspiration, dialect
   - (d.) petition, niche

8. The comedian's _____ was _____ to the audience.
   - (a.) hygiene, luminous
   - (b.) retort, unintelligible
   - (c.) dismay, skeptical
   - (d.) diagnosis, irascible

9. The toddler's _____ caused a(n) _____ in the theater.
   - (a.) nominee, quirk
   - (b.) curiosity, petition
   - (c.) hysteria, upheaval
   - (d.) accessory, retort

10. The _____ aftermath _____ the whole community.
    - (a.) glutton's, tainted
    - (b.) calamity's, astounded
    - (c.) niche's, snared
    - (d.) quirk's, dishonored

Classifying Words

Sort the words in the box by writing each word to complete a phrase in the correct category.

absurd	aspiration	catastrophe	curiosity	dilapidated
effect	elapse	excursions	finicky	glutton
hygiene	hypothesis	inundated	irascible	lyrics
nominee	persuasive	petition	skeptical	swelter

Words You Might Use to Talk About Habits and Quirks

1. has always been _____ about eating vegetables

2. such lively _____ that she asks too many questions

3. joins in on the _____ of every song on the radio

4. practices good _____ so she always looks presentable

5. makes a(n) _____ of himself when strawberries are in season

Words You Might Use to Talk About Vacations

6. visit the site of the historic _____

7. take as many sight-seeing _____ as we can

8. likes to sit on a hot beach and _____

9. _____ us with travel brochures

10. shops for antiques in old, _____ barns

Words You Might Use to Talk About Solving Problems

11. says no idea should ever be called foolish or _____

12. making a(n) _____ about the cause of the problem

13. using words, not fists, to be _____

14. makes every attempt to avoid their _____ classmate

15. letting some time _____ before taking any action

Words You Might Use to Talk About a Political Campaign

16. votes for the best _____ for the job

17. having the _____ of becoming president

18. feeling a little _____ about some of the candidates' promises

19. circulated a(n) _____ to put the issue on the ballot

20. thought about the _____ the candidate would have on our country

CHAPTER 4

WORD LIST

Read each word using the pronunciation key.

accuracy (ak´ yər ə sē)
bauble (bô´ bəl)
caustic (kô´ stik)
decry (di krī´)
dilemma (di lem´ ə)
disown (dis ōn´)
elimination (i lim ə nā´ shən)
external (ek stər´ nəl)
flippant (flip´ ənt)
grieve (grēv)
idolize (īd´ ə līz)
isolate (ī´ sə lāt)
maneuver (mə nōō´ vər)
nonchalant (non shə länt´)
pillar (pil´ ər)
random (ran´ dəm)
rung (ruŋ)
speculate (spek´ yə lāt)
tangible (tan´ jə bəl)
upright (up´ rīt)

WORD STUDY

Prefixes

The prefix *trans-* means "across, over, through," or "beyond."

transatlantic (trans ət lan´ tik) *(adj.)* crossing or reaching across the Atlantic
transcend (tran send´) *(v.)* to rise above
transform (trans fôrm´) *(v.)* to change in form
translate (trans´ lāt) *(v.)* to change from one language into another
translucent (trans lōō´ sənt) *(adj.)* allowing light to pass through partially
transmit (trans mit´) *(v.)* to send, pass along, or communicate

Challenge Words

absolution (ab sə lōō´ shən)
erratic (i rat´ ik)
jocund (jok´ ənd)
magnanimous (mag nan´ ə məs)
tout (tout)

WORDS IN CONTEXT

Read each sentence below to figure out the meaning of the word in **bold**. Use reasoning skills and the remainder of the sentence to help you. Write the meaning of the word on the line.

1. Unable to resolve the **dilemma**, Matt and Ari turned to others for advice.

   _____

2. Liz hurt Ted's feelings with her **caustic** remark about his costume.

   _____

3. As the milk streamed across the table, I ran to put the carton **upright**.

   _____

4. Ashley offered no **tangible** proof that Tony had cheated, so the principal had to believe that he had not.

   _____

5. The townspeople will surely **decry** any decision that might damage the forest.

   _____

6. Ramón threw the darts with great **accuracy** and hit three bull's-eyes in a row.

   _____

7. Kathy's father grounded her for two days for her **flippant** response to her uncle.

   _____

8. The baby likes to play with the **baubles** hanging around her mother's neck.

   _____

9. Among the ruins of the ancient temple, only two stone **pillars** remain.

   _____

10. Brian will probably **grieve** the loss of his iguana for several weeks.

   _____

Chapter 4   Level H

WORD MEANINGS

Word Learning

Study the spelling, part(s) of speech, and meaning(s) of each word. Complete each sentence by writing the word on the line. Then read the sentence.

1. **accuracy** *(n.)* 1. the quality of being correct; 2. exactness

   I did not have much faith in the _____ of my guess.

2. **bauble** *(n.)* a small decoration or trinket

   My friend showed me the new _____ on her wrist.

3. **caustic** *(adj.)* 1. capable of burning, dissolving, or causing other damage; 2. harshly critical or sarcastic

   Scientists often use _____ chemicals in the lab.

4. **decry** *(v.)* 1. to criticize publicly; 2. to devalue

   We were surprised that they did not _____ the senator's plan.

5. **dilemma** *(n.)* a situation that requires a difficult choice

   Kristin faced the _____ of how she would do all that work in two weeks.

6. **disown** *(v.)* to refuse to accept as one's own

   Eddie might _____ the idea rather than take credit for it.

7. **elimination** *(n.)* removal

   They agreed upon the _____ of three items from the menu.

8. **external** *(adj.)* on the outside or outer part

   The house is fine inside, but it has some _____ flaws.

9. **flippant** *(adj.)* lacking respect or seriousness

   The others may not appreciate your _____ attitude because they take the matter very seriously.

10. **grieve** *(v.)* 1. to feel great sadness; 2. to cause great sadness

    The hockey team began to _____ when they learned the spring thaw had melted their hockey rink.

11. **idolize** *(v.)* 1. to view with admiration or devotion; 2. to worship

    I think she will always _____ her mother.

12. **isolate** *(v.)* to separate from a group or whole

    The zookeeper decided to _____ the sick giraffe from the other animals.

13. **maneuver** *(n.)* a planned and skillful move; *(v.)* to make a skillful move

    The skater made a graceful _____ on the ice.

    I can't _____ the fishing pole very well while I'm sitting in the boat.

14. **nonchalant** *(adj.)* not concerned; indifferent

    She appears _____, but I know she is worried about the contest.

15. **pillar** *(n.)* 1. a building column that supports something above, such as a roof; 2. a person in an important position

    A 20-foot _____ stood at each corner of the pavilion.

16. **random** *(adj.)* 1. happening or done without a plan; 2. without order

    Jackie lay the floor tiles in a _____ fashion.

17. **rung** *(n.)* 1. a step of a ladder; 2. the piece of wood that spans two chair legs for support

    Michael stood on the lowest _____ of the ladder.

18. **speculate** *(v.)* 1. to think carefully about or suppose; 2. to buy or sell something in hopes of making a profit

    I _____ that spring will come early this year.

19. **tangible** *(adj.)* able to be seen or touched

    The decision had no _____ effects.

20. **upright** *(adj.)* 1. in a standing, straight-up position; 2. morally good

    She played the tunes on an old _____ piano.

Vocabulary in Action

You already know that a **dilemma** is a problem that offers at least two solutions, none of which are acceptable or ideal. A person who finds herself in a dilemma has been traditionally been described as being placed "on the horns of a dilemma;" that is, neither horn is very comfortable. There are many famous dilemmas. Here are a few you may want to learn more about: Cornelian dilemma, Euthyphro dilemma, Platonia dilemma, Hedgehog's dilemma, and Prisoner's dilemma.

Use Your Vocabulary

Choose the word from the Word List that best completes each sentence. Write the word on the line. You may use the plural form of nouns and the past tense of verbs if necessary.

An ordinary walk to a(n) __1__ creek ended up causing my friends and me to __2__. Instead of natural beauty, we found brown water and dead fish. At first, we sat down and __3__ the sad sight. Then we decided that __4__ of the problem was a better use of our time. We tossed out some __5__ ideas. We __6__ about what we should do. Then we traced our way back along the creek. Soon we came to a factory at the edge of the water. A(n) __7__ pipe ran down the building. It must have had a leak, because __8__ chemicals were pouring into the creek.

That's not the end of the story, though. Now I had a real __9__. The factory was the place where my father worked. Would Dad get in trouble? Would I? My friends and I tried to be __10__ as we asked for the boss, but inside we were shaking. We were afraid she would think we were just a bunch of __11__ troublemakers. She definitely did not! When she heard our story, she called for quick action. A man in protective clothing brought a ladder to the leaky pipe. He braced it between the creek bottom and a(n) __12__ __13__ on the side of the building. He stood on the ladder's bottom __14__ and went to work with skill and __15__. With a few quick __16__, he stopped the leak. My dad's boss breathed a sigh of relief and smiled at my friends and me. I wasn't afraid of her anymore. I __17__ her for her fast thinking.

But I was afraid Dad would __18__ me for all the trouble I'd caused. Instead, he greeted me that night with a big smile. He handed me a necklace with a tiny fish charm. I cherish that necklace. It is not just a(n) __19__. It is a(n) __20__ reminder of the day we saved the creek.

1. _____
2. _____
3. _____
4. _____
5. _____
6. _____
7. _____
8. _____
9. _____
10. _____
11. _____
12. _____
13. _____
14. _____
15. _____
16. _____
17. _____
18. _____
19. _____
20. _____

SYNONYMS

Synonyms are words that have the same or nearly the same meanings.

Part 1 Choose the word from the box that is the best synonym for each group of words. Write the word on the line.

caustic	grieve	decry	pillar
external	flippant	speculate	tangible

1. corroding, acidic, stinging, biting _____

2. mourn, sorrow, distress, pain _____

3. frivolous, offhand, light _____

4. consider, contemplate, to venture _____

5. post, pole, a leader _____

6. physical, real, concrete _____

7. denounce, condemn, to diminish _____

8. outer, exterior _____

Part 2 Replace the underlined word with a word from the box that means the same or almost the same. Write your answer on the line.

upright	bauble	isolate	dilemma
random	disown	maneuver	

9. Matthew feared that his angry grandfather would <u>renounce</u> him.

_____

10. He has a very <u>honest</u> character. _____

11. Every time Courtney tries to finish early, she runs into a <u>jam</u>.

_____

12. The veterinarian chose to <u>quarantine</u> all of the sick animals.

_____

13. John hung a red <u>ornament</u> on the tree. _____

14. The swift military <u>operation</u> surprised the unsuspecting foes.

_____

15. Always be on the lookout for a <u>chance</u> opportunity. _____

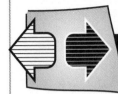 **ANTONYMS**

Antonyms are words that have opposite or nearly opposite meanings.

Part 1 Choose the word from the box that is the best antonym for each group of words. Write the word on the line.

decry	disown	external
idolize	isolate	random

1. claim, accept as one's own   _____

2. compliment, admire, value   _____

3. join, unite, combine   _____

4. deliberate, planned, intentional   _____

5. despise, scorn, disdain   _____

6. inner, internal   _____

Part 2 Replace the underlined word with a word from the box that means the opposite or almost the opposite. Write your answer on the line.

accuracy	flippant	grieve	nonchalant	caustic

7. Jimmy's departure caused everyone to <u>celebrate</u>. _____

8. We were all surprised by Andy's <u>solemn</u> response to the tragedy.

_____

9. Susanna appeared quite <u>emotional</u> when her sister walked into the room.

_____

10. Jody's <u>soothing</u> words did not make me feel much better. _____

11. I completed the test with a high level of <u>error</u>. _____

WORD STUDY

Prefixes Choose a word from the box that belongs with each group of words. Write the word on the line.

transatlantic	transcend	transform
translate	translucent	transmit

1. lampshade, screen _____

2. difficulties, cultural boundaries _____

3. memo, message _____

4. flight, relationship, business _____

5. language, computer program _____

6. object, personality, attitude _____

Vocabulary in Action

See if you can spot the Challenge Word in this poem by William Wordsworth. To what does the word refer in this poem?

The Daffodils
by William Wordsworth

I wandered lonely as a cloud
   That floats on high o'er vales and hills,
When all at once I saw a crowd,
   A host, of golden daffodils;
Beside the lake, beneath the trees,
fluttering and dancing in the breeze.

The waves beside them danced, but they
   Out-did the sparkling waves in glee:
A Poet could not but be gay,
   In such a jocund company:
I gazed—and gazed—but little thought
What wealth the show to me had brought:

Continuous as the stars that shine
   And twinkle on the Milky Way,
They stretched in never-ending line
   Along the margin of a bay:
Ten thousand saw I at a glance,
Tossing their heads in sprightly dance.

For oft, when on my couch I lie
   In vacant or in pensive mood,
They flash upon that inward eye
   Which is the bliss of solitude;
And then my heart with pleasure fills,
And dances with the daffodils.

CHALLENGE WORDS

Word Learning—Challenge!

Study the spelling, part of speech, and meaning(s) of each word. Complete each sentence by writing the word on the line. Then read the sentence.

1. **absolution** *(n.)* 1. forgiveness; 2. freeing from punishment

   She asked the judge for the _____ of her jail sentence.

2. **erratic** *(adj.)* 1. irregular in action; 2. odd

   We have heard only _____ reports of the situation.

3. **jocund** *(adj.)* merry, cheerful, or jolly

   We all like Aunt Lilly's _____ good humor.

4. **magnanimous** *(adj.)* showing a generous or noble spirit

   His _____ offer to give up the house touched us all.

5. **tout** *(v.)* to recommend or praise something highly

   If you ask Terry which computer to buy, she will always _____ her most expensive product.

Use Your Vocabulary—Challenge!

Oil Spill There has been an oil spill off the coast of Alaska. You and your friends join the rescue efforts to save the wildlife. Write a story about your rescue operation. Use the Challenge Words above.

> ## *Vocabulary in Action*
>
> Prefixes and suffixes change the meaning of words and how they function in sentences. Studying words and adding prefixes and suffixes will boost your vocabulary. Look at the vocabulary word *transcend* from this chapter. *Transcend* is a transitive verb that means "to rise above or go beyond the limits of." If you add the suffix *-ent*, you create the word *transcendent*. This adjective describes a person or thing that exceeds usual limits. If you add the suffix *-ence*, you get *transcendence*, a noun that names the quality or state of being transcendent. Other variations on the verb *transcend* include *transcendently* and *transcendental*. Study the other words from this chapter and see how many words you can make from them.

In chemistry, letters are used to represent different chemicals and elements. Equations such as the one below show how elements combine to form compounds:

$$2H_2 + O_2 = 2H_2O$$

This shows how hydrogen (H) and oxygen (O) can be combined to make water.

In word chemistry, you'll see an equation like the one above. The letters in each equation combine to make a vocabulary word. A small number to the right of a letter tells you how many times that letter appears in the word. The clue next to the equation gives you a hint. For example:

ELA + B$_2$U = a bright, shiny thing _____

The small 2 tells you there are two b's in this vocabulary word. Determine how many letters are actually in the word. Then rearrange them and write the answer on the line. The answer to the example is **bauble.**

1. $E_2R + IVG$ = to feel sad   _____

2. $RL_2I + AP$ = a support   _____

3. $C_2TS + UAI$ = able to cause damage   _____

4. $UC_3A_2 + YR$ = exactness   _____

5. $N_3LA_2 + TCOH$ = indifferent   _____

6. $I_3N_2AE + ML + OT$ = removal   _____

7. $ZI_2D + O_4LE - O_3$ = to worship   _____

8. $N_3UG_4R_4 - N_2R_3G_3$ = a step of a ladder   _____

WORD LIST

Read each word using the pronunciation key.

acquit (ə kwit′)
belligerent (bə lij′ ər ənt)
censor (sen′ sər)
defiance (di fī′ əns)
diligence (dil′ i jəns)
dispatch (dis pach′)
embankment (em baŋk′ mənt)
facet (fas′ it)
flourish (flər′ ish)
grudge (gruj)
ilk (ilk)
itemize (ī′ tə mīz)
mediocre (mē dē ō′ kər)
notable (nō′ tə bəl)
pivot (piv′ ət)
rascal (ras′ kəl)
sage (sāj)
sprightly (sprīt′ lē)
taut (tôt)
vacuum (vak′ yo͞om)

WORD STUDY

Suffixes

The suffixes *-ous* and *-ious* mean "characterized by."

ambitious (am bi′ shəs) *(adj.)* characterized by ambition; eager to succeed
glorious (glôr′ ē əs) *(adj.)* characterized by glory or splendor
malicious (mə li′ shəs) *(adj.)* characterized by malice, or ill will
nauseous (nô′ shəs) *(adj.)* characterized by nausea, or sickness
nervous (nər′ vəs) *(adj.)* characterized by nerves or anxiety
voracious (vô rā′ shəs) *(adj.)* characterized by a great appetite

Challenge Words

chide (chīd)
contentious (kən ten′ chəs)
filibuster (fil′ ə bus tər)
hypothetical (hī pə thet′ i kəl)
invincible (in vin′ sə bəl)

WORDS IN CONTEXT

Read each sentence below to figure out the meaning of the word in **bold**. Use reasoning skills and the remainder of the sentence to help you. Write the meaning of the word on the line.

1. Matt held the tent ropes **taut** so Deanna could hammer the stakes into the ground.

   _____

2. Keith and his studious friends are all of the same **ilk**.

   _____

3. A lot of people like that new restaurant, but I found the food **mediocre** at best.

   _____

4. Famous actors, **notable** journalists, and politicians filled the audience.

   _____

5. Confucius was a **sage** of ancient China whose sayings are still repeated today.

   _____

6. Michael's departure created a **vacuum** that was not easy to fill.

   _____

7. Notice how the **facets** of the gem reflect the sunlight.

   _____

8. Don't hold a **grudge** against me just because I told your secret.

   _____

9. A lot of inspiration and much **diligence** helped Thomas Edison achieve his status as a great inventor.

   _____

10. Armadillos are everywhere; they **flourish** in warm, dry parts of the country.

    _____

Chapter 5   Level H

WORD MEANINGS

Word Learning

Study the spelling, part(s) of speech, and meaning(s) of each word. Complete each sentence by writing the word on the line. Then read the sentence.

1. **acquit** *(v.)* to find not guilty or free from a charge

   Lack of evidence led the jury to _____ him of the crime.

2. **belligerent** *(adj.)* 1. ready to fight; angry; 2. at war

   She received a _____ letter from her neighbors, demanding that she mow her lawn.

3. **censor** *(n.)* a person who examines materials to remove parts that do not meet a set of standards; *(v.)* to examine for the purpose of removing material that does not meet a set of standards

   The _____ removed everything having to do with crime.

   According to the First Amendment, the government may not

   _____ the press.

4. **defiance** *(n.)* a resistance to authority or an opposing force

   Yolanda stood up in _____ of the bully to defend her sister.

5. **diligence** *(n.)* 1. careful attention to one's job; 2. persistence

   When Josh saw the A on his test, he knew that his _____ had paid off.

6. **dispatch** *(v.)* to send off; *(n.)* 1. act of sending off; 2. speed; 3. a quickly sent written message

   The general will _____ an order to cease firing.

   We received the general's _____ this morning.

7. **embankment** *(n.)* a mound of earth used to prevent flooding or to support a roadway

   When the car hit the icy patch, it swerved up on the _____.

8. **facet** *(n.)* 1. the small, flat surface on a tooth, stone, or gem; 2. a part or phase

   That is a _____ of her personality I have never seen.

9. **flourish** *(v.)* to grow well or thrive

   Despite the lack of nuts and seeds, the squirrels continue to _____.

10. **grudge** *(v.)* to hesitate to give or admit something; *(n.)* a strong feeling of ill will or resentment

They did not _____ me the prize I deserved.

She has always held a _____ against me.

11. **ilk** *(n.)* type or kind

Because she lies, I don't want her _____ hanging around here.

12. **itemize** *(v.)* to list one by one

Please _____ the supplies in the art room.

13. **mediocre** *(adj.)* 1. not good or bad; 2. commonplace

That theater group only produces _____ plays.

14. **notable** *(adj.)* 1. worthy of notice or remarkable; 2. prominent; *(n.)* a person who is worthy of notice

Aside from a broken window, the fire caused no _____ damage.

At the meeting, we saw Ms. Broucek, a _____ in city politics.

15. **pivot** *(n.)* a rod or shaft around which some other part rotates or swings; *(v.)* to rotate or swing

Do you want me to fix the broken _____ on this swing set?

The gymnast will _____ before she reaches the end of the mat.

16. **rascal** *(n.)* a mischievous person or animal

It looks like some furry _____ has gotten into the trash.

17. **sage** *(adj.)* wise or showing keen judgment; *(n.)* 1. a wise person; 2. an herb used for cooking

I appreciate your _____ advice.

Mom brought some fresh _____ home from Billy's garden.

18. **sprightly** *(adj.)* lively, active, or animated

His _____ step showed me that his mood had improved.

19. **taut** *(adj.)* 1. pulled or drawn tight; 2. emotionally or mentally strained or tense

You have to pull the canvas _____ over the frame.

20. **vacuum** *(n.)* 1. a completely empty space; 2. an absence or emptiness; 3. a machine for cleaning by use of suction; *(adj.)* containing air or other gas at reduced pressure

The president's resignation has created a leadership _____.

The company sells _____-packed coffee.

Use Your Vocabulary

Choose the word from the Word List that best completes each sentence. Write the word on the line. You may use the plural form of nouns and the past tense of verbs if necessary.

I am known in my neighborhood as the **1** of Bassett Lane. I earned that title by solving mysteries. One day my friend Brady **2** an urgent message. His new sweater was missing, and he needed to find it.

"That sweater was a gift from Grandma," he said in a(n) **3** voice. "If I don't wear it, her feelings will be hurt."

"That sweater did not just disappear into a(n) **4** ," I said. "When did you last have it?"

Brady couldn't remember, so I asked him to **5** the places he had been. Finally, he recalled leaving it on a chair in his room. I searched the room with **6** . It was very clean, but I did manage to find a few long golden hairs and some tiny pieces of dried mud near the chair. Brady's room, I thought, looked **7** . It was not filled with interesting things like mine. But he did have one **8** decoration. It was a large framed photo of a beautiful dog. "Is that your dog?" I asked.

"Yes," he said proudly. "That's my golden retriever, Toby."

I did not **9** my words. "Toby is the criminal," I declared.

"No way!" Brady answered in a(n) **10** voice, but he followed when I **11** and headed out the door. Outside, I saw muddy paw prints. We followed them down the **12** in the backyard, moving at a(n) **13** pace. Soon we saw Toby lying in front of a small hollow in the bank. Toby stood up with an air of **14** , but when he moved aside, we could see a ball, an old shoe, and other things of that **15** . "Toby's life of crime has **16** ," I laughed. "If you look in there, you will find your sweater." And of course, Brady did.

Toby has not been **17** , but luckily Brady doesn't hold a(n) **18** . He knows playfulness is a(n) **19** of Toby's personality. "You **20** ," he said, petting Toby's head. "From now on, I'll remember to put my things away."

1. _____

2. _____

3. _____

4. _____

5. _____

6. _____

7. _____

8. _____

9. _____

10. _____

11. _____

12. _____

13. _____

14. _____

15. _____

16. _____

17. _____

18. _____

19. _____

20. _____

SYNONYMS

Synonyms are words that have the same or nearly the same meanings.

Part 1 Choose the word from the box that is the best synonym for each group of words. Write the word on the line.

defiance	diligence	dispatch	flourish
itemize	mediocre	rascal	taut

1. transmit, bulletin, quickness _____

2. list, detail, catalog _____

3. rigid, strained, stretched _____

4. prankster, scoundrel, scamp _____

5. ordinary, normal, average _____

6. prosper, succeed _____

7. opposition, disobedience, contempt _____

8. persistence, industriousness, effort _____

Part 2 Replace the underlined word with a word from the box that means the same or almost the same. Write your answer on the line.

belligerent	acquit	censor	sprightly
sage	notable	grudge	

9. The basketball coach chose Melissa for her <u>extraordinary</u> strength.

_____

10. He blamed the problem on his <u>aggressive</u> neighbors. _____

11. Zeke always consulted the old <u>philosopher</u> for advice. _____

12. The two families don't speak to each other because of a long-standing <u>argument</u>.

_____

13. Do you think the judiciary council will <u>pardon</u> her? _____

14. My grandfather is a <u>spry</u> old man. _____

15. The film's obscene language did not get past the <u>inspector</u>. _____

ANTONYMS

Antonyms are words that have opposite or nearly opposite meanings.

Part 1 Choose the word from the box that is the best antonym for each group of words. Write the word on the line.

acquit	flourish	sage	taut	sprightly

1. dull, lethargic, lifeless _____

2. slack, flexible, loose _____

3. fade, decline, fail _____

4. fool, idiot; stupid, senseless _____

5. charge, blame, indict _____

Part 2 Replace the underlined word with a word from the box that means the opposite or almost the opposite. Write your answer on the line.

belligerent	diligence	mediocre	notable

6. Yesterday we saw the <u>outstanding</u> doll exhibit at the museum.

_____

7. She always comes to meetings with a <u>friendly</u> attitude. _____

8. Marco displayed great <u>carelessness</u> in all of his work. _____

9. Medgar Evers was a <u>regular</u> figure in the civil rights movement.

_____

WORD STUDY

Suffixes Choose the word from the box that might be used to describe each person or event. Write the word on the line.

ambitious	glorious	malicious
nauseous	nervous	voracious

1. someone auditioning for a school play   _____

2. a passenger on a bumpy boat ride   _____

3. someone sitting down to Thanksgiving dinner   _____

4. the birth of a child   _____

5. a villain   _____

6. a political campaign   _____

Vocabulary in Action

Look at each word on the Word Study list and try to figure out its noun form. For example, *ambition* is the nominative form of the word ***ambitious.*** Pay attention to how spelling is affected when you change the way a word functions in a sentence.

CHALLENGE WORDS

Word Learning—Challenge!

Study the spelling, part of speech, and meaning of each word. Complete each sentence by writing the word on the line. Then read the sentence.

1. **chide** *(v.)* to voice disapproval in a mild way

   My father always used to _____ me for my impatience.

2. **contentious** *(adj.)* quick to argue or quarrel

   Those kids are a _____ bunch.

3. **filibuster** *(v.)* to attempt to keep a bill from passing in a legislature by the use of excessive speeches

   If it looks like the bill is going to pass, the senator will _____.

4. **hypothetical** *(adj.)* based on an unproved idea

   Tell me about this _____ life on Mars.

5. **invincible** *(adj.)* incapable of being overcome or beaten

   The girls on the soccer team consider themselves _____.

Use Your Vocabulary—Challenge!

Mock Trial Your best friend has been accused of a crime he or she did not commit. You and your classmates hold a mock trial to see if your friend is guilty. On a separate sheet of paper, write about the events that happen. Include the five Challenge Words above. Use your imagination!

Vocabulary in Action

A **filibuster**, or "talking out a bill," is a form of obstruction in a legislature or other decision-making body. The term first came into use in the United States Senate. Senate rules permit a senator to speak for as long as he or she wishes on any topic. A supermajority of three-fifths of the Senate is required to stop a filibuster.

Perhaps the most famous example of a filibuster in American cinema comes from the 1939 film *Mr. Smith Goes to Washington*. At the movie's climax, a young senator—Jefferson Smith, played by Jimmy Stewart—stages a filibuster after he discovers that his mentor is corrupt.

FUN WITH WORDS

Each sentence contains a word from the Word list. As you read each question, think about what you can do to make the world a better place. Write your answers on the lines.

1. What do you think is the most *notable* part of our planet?

   _____

   _____

   _____

2. What can you do to help our planet *flourish*?

   _____

   _____

   _____

3. What *facets* of our world would you change? Why?

   _____

   _____

   _____

4. *Itemize* at least five things that you enjoy about the world we live in.

   _____

   _____

   _____

5. If you could *dispatch* a message to people in the past, what would you ask them to do to protect the world we live in today?

   _____

   _____

   _____

   _____

WORD LIST

Read each word using the pronunciation key.

admissible (ad mis´ ə bəl)
beneficial (ben ə fish´ əl)
colleague (kol´ ēg)
deflate (di flāt´)
dilute (dī loot´)
dispense (di spens´)
emotional (i mō´ shə nəl)
fallow (fal´ ō)
fluted (floo´ tid)
haphazard (hap haz´ ərd)
illustrious (i lus´ trē əs)
jaunt (jônt)
merit (mâr´ it)
notorious (nō tôr´ ē əs)
platform (plat´ fôrm)
ratify (rat´ ə fī)
saline (sā´ lēn)
squander (skwon´ dər)
tenacity (tə nas´ ə tē)
venture (ven´ chər)

WORD STUDY

Homophones

Homophones are words that sound alike but have different spellings and meanings. Study the pairs of homophones below.

altar (ôl´ tər) *(n.)* a platform or raised area, as in a church
alter (ôl´ tər) *(v.)* to change

raise (rāz´) *(v.)* 1. to lift something; 2. to grow or breed something
raze (rāz´) *(v.)* to demolish

reek (rēk´) *(n.)* a terrible smell; *(v.)* to smell terrible
wreak (rēk´) *(v.)* to cause

Challenge Words

angst (äŋkst)
egocentric (ē gō sen´ trik)
fluctuate (fluk´ choo āt)
obtrusive (əb troo´ siv)
vindicate (vin´ di kāt)

WORDS IN CONTEXT

Read each sentence below to figure out the meaning of the word in **bold**. Use reasoning skills and the remainder of the sentence to help you. Write the meaning of the word on the line.

1. Your aunt is a senator? I never knew you had such **illustrious** relatives.

_____

2. Representatives from both countries met today to **ratify** the new trade agreement.

_____

3. As I watched the pilot **deflate** the hot-air balloon, I thought about how much fun I'd had up in the air.

_____

4. I'm sure you've heard of Mr. Lane, the man who is **notorious** for his bad jokes.

_____

5. Use water to **dilute** the concentrated juice.

_____

6. He warned his sister not to **squander** her summer earnings on ice cream and movies.

_____

7. Janice waited impatiently on the **platform** for her brother's train.

_____

8. The fisherman's **tenacity** finally paid off when he caught the big fish after standing knee-deep in water all day.

_____

9. The **saline** solution in the beaker is for the next experiment.

_____

10. With Halloween pranksters everywhere, Kyle knew better than to **venture** outside the house.

_____

© Loyola Press.

WORD MEANINGS

Word Learning

Study the spelling, part(s) of speech, and meaning(s) of each word. Complete each sentence by writing the word on the line. Then read the sentence.

1. **admissible** *(adj.)* 1. acceptable; 2. worthy of being permitted

    A hunch is not considered _____ evidence.

2. **beneficial** *(adj.)* 1. making better or having benefit; 2. helpful

    Would it be _____ to talk to other people who know about this?

3. **colleague** *(n.)* a fellow worker

    Harold was my _____ when I worked for the law firm.

4. **deflate** *(v.)* 1. to release air or gas from; 2. to reduce confidence or value

    If you tell her the bad news, you will _____ her hopes completely.

5. **dilute** *(v.)* to thin or weaken by adding liquid; *(adj.)* weakened

    What should I use to _____ this paint?

    We used a very _____ solution for the experiment.

6. **dispense** *(v.)* 1. to give out or distribute; 2. to release from a duty

    I can't get the machine to _____ the candy properly.

7. **emotional** *(adj.)* with strong feeling

    Our principal delivered a very _____ graduation speech.

8. **fallow** *(adj.)* 1. plowed or tilled but not seeded for one growing season; 2. uncultivated; *(n.)* earth that is plowed but not seeded

    We won't plant our _____ land until next year.

    Sara and Mark are out plowing the _____ today.

9. **fluted** *(adj.)* decorated with grooves

    For my birthday, I received a lovely pair of _____ water glasses.

10. **haphazard** *(adj.)* by chance or without planning

    Her _____ attempts to organize the room were unsuccessful.

11. **illustrious** *(adj.)* well-known, famous

    The princess and her _____ guests danced all night long.

12. **jaunt** *(n.)* a short trip

I'll just take a _____ down to the beach.

13. **merit** *(n.)* a valuable quality or trait; *(v.)* to earn or deserve

These scholarships are based on _____.

I thought he did not _____ such fine praise.

14. **notorious** *(adj.)* well-known, usually for unfavorable reasons

Have you seen the _____ robber?

15. **platform** *(n.)* 1. a raised surface; 2. the deck of a train station; 3. the ideas of a political candidate or party

City parking reform is an important part of the candidate's _____.

16. **ratify** *(v.)* to approve for use or action

Congress did not _____ the new amendment to the Constitution.

17. **saline** *(adj.)* of, relating to, or containing salt

We cannot drink the ocean's _____ waters.

18. **squander** *(v.)* to spend wastefully

She feared that her son would _____ all of his hard-earned money.

19. **tenacity** *(n.)* firmness, persistence, or determination

Eleanor showed _____ and grit when she chose to stay on the farm alone through the entire winter.

20. **venture** *(n.)* 1. a task that is risky or dangerous; 2. an undertaking involving chance; *(v.)* 1. to expose to danger; 2. to risk or to brave; 3. to offer at risk of rejection

Marty lost some money in that business _____.

I don't even want to _____ a guess about what happened.

Use Your Vocabulary

Choose the word from the Word List that best completes each sentence. Write the word on the line. You may use the plural form of nouns and the past tense of verbs if necessary.

When it came time to organize the spring dance, few students __1__ to get involved. We were all glad when Kendra decided to take charge. She had the __2__ to whip the student council into shape. The council was __3__ for sitting like a(n) __4__ field and producing very little. We had pulled off the last dance in a very __5__ fashion, and no one had much fun. Kendra leaped into her role as the boss and set up an operating budget for the dance.

"We can't __6__ our limited funds," she said. "We don't need a machine to __7__ the drinks. We'll just make lemonade in pitchers." She thought it __8__ to organize very carefully. We found her plan __9__ and __10__ all of her proposals.

Jake, one of our __11__ on Student Council, suggested the theme of ancient Greece. We borrowed some __12__ plastic columns from the drama club and transformed the gym into an ancient Greek temple. We built a(n) __13__ at one end of the gym, where two students would be crowned as Apollo and Athena.

We all came to school early on the big day to start blowing up balloons. I was a little concerned that they might __14__ over the course of the day, but they didn't. Late in the day, Kendra sent Mandy on a(n) __15__ to the store to pick up the lemonade. When Mandy returned, she __16__ the concentrate with water and took a sip. She made a horrible face. "Oh no! This is too sour!" she cried out. Mandy tended to get fairly __17__ about things.

"Don't worry," said Kendra. "I saw a bowl of sugar in the cafeteria." She brought back a bowl of white crystallized powder and dumped it into the punch bowl. Mandy had another sip, and made an even more horrible face. I tried it myself, and it had a distinctly __18__ taste.

"Kendra," I said. "That bowl was full of salt!"

Salty lemonade aside, the dance was a success. All agreed that Kendra __19__ great praise for putting together the most __20__ event of the school year.

1. _____
2. _____
3. _____
4. _____
5. _____
6. _____
7. _____
8. _____
9. _____
10. _____
11. _____
12. _____
13. _____
14. _____
15. _____
16. _____
17. _____
18. _____
19. _____
20. _____

SYNONYMS

Synonyms are words that have the same or nearly the same meanings.

Part 1 Choose the word from the box that is the best synonym for each group of words. Write the word on the line.

admissible	colleague	dilute	haphazard
jaunt	merit	ratify	venture

1. random, unplanned, not systematic _____

2. worth, quality; be entitled to _____

3. allowable, legitimate _____

4. endorse, support, agree to _____

5. excursion, trip _____

6. watered down; make less thick _____

7. associate, teammate, partner _____

8. hazard; imperil, endanger _____

Part 2 Replace the underlined word(s) with a word from the box that means the same or almost the same. Write your answer on the line.

fallow	notorious	emotional	platform
illustrious	beneficial	squander	

9. We held our rally on a huge wooden <u>stage</u>. _____

10. I am honored to have such a(n) <u>celebrated</u> author in our midst.

    _____

11. He proceeded to <u>throw away</u> his money on expensive cars and extravagant vacations.

    _____

12. It would be <u>advantageous</u> to research your options before making a purchase.

    _____

13. I found myself in the midst of a(n) <u>passionate</u> debate. _____

14. Her mind lay <u>inactive</u> for many years. _____

15. I dreaded the <u>infamous</u> Midwestern winter. _____

 **ANTONYMS**

Antonyms are words that have opposite or nearly opposite meanings.

Part 1 Choose the word from the box that is the best antonym for each group of words. Write the word on the line.

merit	venture	squander	haphazard	beneficial

1. safety, security; protect _____

2. organized, methodical, designed _____

3. useless, harmful, detrimental _____

4. fault, defect; not to be worthy of _____

5. save, use wisely _____

Part 2 Replace the underlined word with a word from the box that means the opposite or almost the opposite. Write your answer on the line.

tenacity	emotional	ratify	admissible	dilute

6. The committee would not <u>veto</u> the proposal. _____

7. The illness really did <u>intensify</u> her strength. _____

8. I have never heard such an <u>unfeeling</u> argument for kindness to animals.

_____

9. As our leader, he showed more <u>indecision</u> than usual. _____

10. The university judged the research findings <u>unacceptable</u>. _____

WORD STUDY

Homophones Choose the word from the box that best completes each of the following sentences.

raise	alter	wreak
raze	altar	reek

1. She refuses to _____ the way she does things.

2. Tom's locker began to _____ on Monday because he left his gym shoes in it over the weekend.

3. The workers will _____ the barn that was destroyed by the fire.

4. Spilled liquids will _____ havoc with the computer keyboard.

5. The newly married couple walked all the way around the _____.

6. If you call her name, she will _____ her head.

Vocabulary in Action

The word **angst**, a Germanic word meaning "fear" or "anxiety," is a fairly new addition to the English language. British writer George Eliot used the word as early as 1849, and it was popularized in English by translations of Sigmund Freud's work. But *angst* was not considered an English word until the 1940s. It is used in English to describe "an intense feeling of emotional strife." The German definition of *angst* is "the fear of possible suffering and a behavior resulting from uncertainty and strain which is caused by pain, loss, or death." In German, angst is different from fear in that fear usually refers to a material threat while angst is a nondirectional emotion.

CHALLENGE WORDS

Word Learning—Challenge!

Study the spelling, part of speech, and meaning(s) of each word. Complete each sentence by writing the word on the line. Then read the sentence.

1. **angst** *(n.)* anxiety or apprehension

   Travis thought about the upcoming events with great _____.

2. **egocentric** *(n.)* 1. being concerned with the individual rather than society; 2. self-centered; selfish

   I find her _____ and difficult to work with.

3. **fluctuate** *(v.)* 1. to continually change between two choices; 2. to vary

   Gasoline prices will probably continue to _____.

4. **obtrusive** *(adj.)* calling attention to manner or conduct in an undesirable way

   Your _____ remarks are making it hard for us to discuss this rationally.

5. **vindicate** *(v.)* 1. to free from blame; 2. to justify; 3. to uphold

   If I can prove I was right, I am hoping to _____ myself.

Use Your Vocabulary—Challenge!

Committee Plans Now it's time for your school to plan a week-long festival of sports and cultural events. But the members of the student planning committee cannot decide how to run things. Use the five Challenge Words above to write a story describing the events leading up to the festival.

> ### Vocabulary in Action
>
> Did you know that the word *homonym* comes from the conjunction of the Greek prefix *homo-*, meaning "same," and the suffix *-onym*, meaning "name"? Thus, it refers to two or more distinct words sharing the "same name."

FUN WITH WORDS

Complete the crossword puzzle using words from the Word List.

Across

3. showing feelings
6. acceptable
7. tilled but not seeded
8. famous
10. determination
11. to reduce confidence
12. to weaken
13. a quick trip

Down

1. to deserve
2. infamous
4. an associate
5. to approve
7. with grooves
9. salty

Review 4–6

Word Meanings Fill in the bubble of the word that is best defined by each phrase.

1. not planned
   - **a.** haphazard
   - **b.** notorious
   - **c.** mediocre
   - **d.** flippant

2. to use wastefully
   - **a.** deflate
   - **b.** squander
   - **c.** decry
   - **d.** grieve

3. a learned person
   - **a.** embankment
   - **b.** sage
   - **c.** colleague
   - **d.** rascal

4. to clear from an accusation
   - **a.** itemize
   - **b.** disown
   - **c.** dispatch
   - **d.** acquit

5. celebrated and noted
   - **a.** caustic
   - **b.** emotional
   - **c.** illustrious
   - **d.** sprightly

6. to officially approve and confirm
   - **a.** speculate
   - **b.** ratify
   - **c.** dispense
   - **d.** deflate

7. to prosper
   - **a.** flourish
   - **b.** grieve
   - **c.** isolate
   - **d.** itemize

8. to direct or enact skillfully
   - **a.** idolize
   - **b.** maneuver
   - **c.** pivot
   - **d.** squander

9. not outstanding
   - **a.** external
   - **b.** fallow
   - **c.** dilute
   - **d.** mediocre

10. carefree and unconcerned
    - **a.** upright
    - **b.** taut
    - **c.** nonchalant
    - **d.** haphazard

11. elevated flooring
    - **a.** pillar
    - **b.** embankment
    - **c.** platform
    - **d.** dilemma

12. a showy ornament of little value
    - **a.** bauble
    - **b.** sage
    - **c.** vacuum
    - **d.** elimination

13. to be reluctant to give
    - **a.** censor
    - **b.** merit
    - **c.** grudge
    - **d.** disown

14. can be allowed
    - **a.** flippant
    - **b.** beneficial
    - **c.** admissible
    - **d.** emotional

15. a class or sort of something
    - **a.** facet
    - **b.** ilk
    - **c.** colleague
    - **d.** tenacity

16. hostile and inclined to fight
    - **a.** saline
    - **b.** emotional
    - **c.** external
    - **d.** belligerent

17. to disapprove strongly
  (a.) ratify   **(b.)** isolate   **(c.)** decry   **(d.)** venture

18. a brief outing
  (a.) jaunt   **(b.)** grudge   **(c.)** dispatch   **(d.)** diligence

19. that which can be touched
  (a.) illustrious   **(b.)** fluted   **(c.)** random   **(d.)** tangible

20. a vertical support structure
  (a.) pillar   **(b.)** bauble   **(c.)** accuracy   **(d.)** rung

Sentence Completion Choose the word from the box that best completes each of the following sentences. Write the word in the blank.

dilute	dilemma	dispensed	upright	censored
facets	defiance	random	notable	merits

1. Leticia faced a(n) _____ when two people asked her to the dance.

2. Our local museum contains many _____ sculptures.

3. Scientists could find no pattern to the animals' behavior, so they concluded the bears' actions must be _____.

4. During World War II, all mail to and from soldiers was _____ to make sure no national secrets were being revealed.

5. Jack _____ the supplies and showed us how to pack them.

6. The many _____ of the stone reflected the light.

7. Tom's hard work on the play's stage _____ recognition.

8. Because the tent was small, Jan found it impossible to stand _____.

9. _____ of the rules will get you in trouble.

10. A(n) _____ solution of vinegar and water makes a good cleanser.

Fill in the Blanks Fill in the bubble of the pair of words that best completes each sentence.

1. Every year a(n) _____ citizen of our town is awarded "_____ of the Community."
  (a.) upright, Rascal   **(c.)** sprightly, Bauble
  (b.) illustrious, Pillar   **(d.)** belligerent, Censor

2. Make sure the tightrope is _____ before you _____ out on it.
  a. notable, maneuver
  b. deflated, jaunt
  c. mediocre, pivot
  d. taut, venture

3. Even though the jury _____ him, he would always remain _____ to the villagers.
  a. idolized, nonchalant
  b. acquitted, notorious
  c. dispatched, sage
  d. censored, sprightly

4. My _____ and I find sharing ideas _____.
  a. baubles, fluted
  b. pillars, admissible
  c. colleagues, beneficial
  d. rascals, belligerent

5. Everyone agrees that Betsy's hard work on the project _____ a(n) _____ reward.
  a. deflates, fallow
  b. acquits, beneficial
  c. merits, tangible
  d. grieves, emotional

6. It's fun to _____ about ways to _____ a million dollars.
  a. isolate, disown
  b. maneuver, itemize
  c. decry, dispense
  d. speculate, squander

7. In the game of basketball, it is _____ to _____ with the ball, but not to walk with it.
  a. admissible, pivot
  b. beneficial, jaunt
  c. flippant, upkeep
  d. mediocre, dispatch

8. Your _____ attitude won't help solve our _____.
  a. notable, maneuver
  b. belligerent, dilemma
  c. external, elimination
  d. emotional, tenacity

9. The tropical fish will _____ in a tank filled with _____ water.
  a. maneuver, fallow
  b. grieve, sprightly
  c. flourish, saline
  d. venture, admissible

10. Lily should learn to _____ her _____ remarks before she speaks.
  a. censor, caustic
  b. acquit, fluted
  c. isolate, external
  d. itemize, flippant

Classifying Words

Sort the words in the box by writing each word to complete a phrase in the correct category.

accuracy	baubles	belligerent	colleague	defiance
dilute	dispensed	elimination	external	grudge
isolate	maneuver	nonchalant	pillar	platform
random	rung	tangible	upright	vacuum

Words You Might Use to Talk About Attitudes

1. trying to act calm and _____ when you're really nervous
2. getting into fights because of his _____ attitude
3. looks like _____ but really is shyness
4. bitter because she can't stop holding a(n) _____
5. the _____ person who always tries to do the right thing

Words You Might Use to Talk About Ways to Earn Money

6. designing pretty _____ to sell at craft fairs
7. offering to do _____ chores for your neighbors
8. run the _____ cleaner and wash dishes
9. always more fun to work with a(n) _____
10. proud when you've earned a(n) _____ reward

Words You Might Use to Talk About Construction

11. paint or aluminum siding on the _____ walls
12. _____ long boards around without knocking people down
13. a porch with a(n) _____ on each side of the door
14. making sure each _____ of the ladder is unbroken and tight
15. beginning the deck by building a(n) _____

Words You Might Use to Talk About Science Experiments

16. figure out a way to _____ each variable
17. recording results with perfect _____
18. water to _____ a solution that is too strong
19. using chemicals only when _____ by your teacher
20. _____ of a hypothesis you've proved incorrect

WORD LIST

Read each word using the pronunciation key.

affect (ə fekt´)
benign (bi nīn´)
commencement (kə mens´ mənt)
dehydration (dē hī drā´ shən)
dimension (di men´ shən)
disposal (dis pō´ zəl)
endear (en dēr´)
falter (fôl´ tər)
forage (fôr´ ij)
harness (här´ nis)
immortality (im môr tal´ i tē)
jollity (jol´ i tē)
mete (mēt)
novelty (nov´ əl tē)
platoon (plə to͞on´)
rebuttal (ri but´ əl)
savory (sā´ və rē)
squelch (skwelch)
torrent (tôr´ ent)
vertical (vər´ ti kəl)

WORD STUDY

Root Words

The Latin roots *spec*, and *spect* mean "to look" or "to look at."

expect (ek spekt´) *(v.)* 1. to look out for; 2. to anticipate
inspect (in spekt´) *(v.)* to look into or examine carefully
prospect (prä´ spekt) *(n.)* 1. something that is awaited or expected; 2. a possibility; 3. a vision
respect (ri spekt´) *(v.)* to honor or treat with esteem
spectacle (spek´ tə kəl) *(n.)* something held to public view
spectator (spek´ tā tər) *(n.)* someone who looks on or watches

Challenge Words

berate (bi rāt´)
divisive (di vī´ siv)
lucrative (lo͞o´ krə tiv)
meticulous (mə tik´ yə ləs)
pugnacious (pug nā´ shəs)

WORDS IN CONTEXT

Read each sentence below to figure out the meaning of the word in **bold**. Use reasoning skills and the remainder of the sentence to help you. Write the meaning of the word on the line.

1. Some cities would like to **harness** the sun's power and convert it to electricity.

   _____

2. What will **affect** your decision whether or not to try out for the soccer team?

   _____

3. The bus driver quickly **squelched** our noisy singing.

   _____

4. The school is planning to hold the **commencement** activities outside.

   _____

5. Newspaper **disposal** is easier with the new recycling program.

   _____

6. The river rose in a **torrent** after last week's rain.

   _____

7. **Savory** aromas drifted out of the cookie shop.

   _____

8. The candidate's **rebuttal** to her opponent's remarks will appear in tomorrow's newspaper.

   _____

9. We wrote the room **dimensions** on paper so that we would know how much carpet to buy.

   _____

10. During the winter months, all kinds of wildlife **forage** in our backyard.

    _____

WORD MEANINGS

Word Learning

Study the spelling, part(s) of speech, and meaning(s) of each word. Complete each sentence by writing the word on the line. Then read the sentence.

1. **affect** *(v.)* 1. to make something change; 2. to pretend

   The bad weather did not _____ his mood.

2. **benign** *(adj.)* gentle or harmless

   We found the mix-up to be a _____ mistake.

3. **commencement** *(n.)* 1. a beginning; 2. a ceremony for graduation

   She looked forward to the _____ of the basketball season.

4. **dehydration** *(n.)* the removal or loss of water

   The apples shriveled and withered because of _____.

5. **dimension** *(n.)* a measure of length, width, or height

   Which _____ of the box is too big?

6. **disposal** *(n.)* removal or getting rid of

   Our city treats waste _____ as a serious issue.

7. **endear** *(v.)* to make dear or fond of

   Her whines and pleas did not _____ her to me.

8. **falter** *(v.)* 1. to hesitate; 2. to lapse in confidence; *(n.)* 1. unsure action; 2. quavering sound

   I will stand tall and never _____.

   I heard the _____ in his voice.

9. **forage** *(n.)* 1. food for animals; 2. a search for food or provisions; *(v.)* to search for food

   What do the birds do for winter _____?

   Hansel and Gretel had to _____ in the woods for their dinner.

10. **harness** *(n.)* the straps used on an animal to help it pull something; *(v.)* 1. to bring under control; 2. to utilize

    The horse struggled when placed in its _____.

    People use windmills to _____ the wind's power.

11. **immortality** *(n.)* 1. living forever; 2. lasting fame

    In Greek mythology, the gods sometimes granted _____ to human beings.

12. **jollity** *(n.)* 1. a happy feeling; 2. merriment

    The singing and games created a tone of _____ at the dinner table.

13. **mete** *(v.)* 1. to give out; 2. to distribute

    The council will _____ out a fitting punishment.

14. **novelty** *(n.)* 1. something new, unusual, or original; 2. newness

    My sister found the laughing duck quite a _____.

15. **platoon** *(n.)* 1. division within a military company; 2. any group of people working together

    They belonged to the same _____ when they were in the army.

16. **rebuttal** *(n.)* the offering of opposing evidence or arguments

    The professor offered no _____ to my comment.

17. **savory** *(adj.)* having a pleasant taste or smell; *(n.)* one of a group of herbs used for cooking

    We ate a salad with a most _____ dressing.

    Did you put _____ in the soup?

18. **squelch** *(v.)* 1. to stop; 2. to put down with a remark; *(n.)* a harsh reply

    The strict measures tended to _____ the workers' creativity.

    I could not ignore her stinging _____ of my idea.

19. **torrent** *(n.)* 1. a raging flood; 2. any constant, strong flow

    A _____ of shouts and cries greeted her as soon as she opened the window.

20. **vertical** *(adj.)* 1. lengthwise; 2. straight up and down or upright

    The _____ length of the curtain exceeds that of the window.

Use Your Vocabulary

Choose the word from the Word List that best completes each sentence. Write the word on the line. You may use the plural form of nouns and the past tense of verbs if necessary.

Germany invaded Poland in 1939, marking the __1__ of World War II. This invasion seriously __2__ other nations. Led by Adolf Hitler, Germany invaded neighboring countries. People quickly realized that Hitler was anything but a(n) __3__ influence in Europe. At first, the United States waited to see if other countries could __4__ Hitler's aggressions. However, when Germany's ally, Japan, bombed Pearl Harbor, the United States entered the war and sent thousands of __5__ abroad.

The war was difficult for the soldiers. Some marched through __6__ of rain in jungle climates, while others suffered from __7__ in the deserts. Officers tried to __8__ out supplies fairly, but food was often scarce. At times, soldiers had to __9__ and eat whatever food they could find. Many dreamed of the __10__ meals they had enjoyed at home. Getting rest was difficult too. Some soldiers learned to sleep in a(n) __11__ position so that they could be ready to move at any moment.

Famous entertainers would visit the army camps to bring soldiers a touch of laughter and __12__. The sight of people in civilian clothes was a(n) __13__ and provided a boost to the soldiers' spirits.

Americans at home rarely __14__ in their attempts to help the war effort. Many people worked in factories, planted gardens, rationed food, and managed the __15__ and recycling of such materials as metal and rubber. Some women __16__ themselves to soldiers by writing and sending news from home. Some soldiers gained __17__ through their heroic deeds. Without the efforts of these soldiers, the war would have been lost.

After the war ended on May 8, 1945, negotiations for a peace treaty took place. Discussions about the new __18__ of countries and territories often turned into disagreements. Finally, after a series of proposals and __19__, a treaty was written and signed. As part of the peace agreement, the United Nations was formed to help __20__ any future aggression between nations.

1. _____
2. _____
3. _____
4. _____
5. _____
6. _____
7. _____
8. _____
9. _____
10. _____
11. _____
12. _____
13. _____
14. _____
15. _____
16. _____
17. _____
18. _____
19. _____
20. _____

SYNONYMS

Synonyms are words that have the same or nearly the same meanings.

Part 1 Choose the word from the box that is the best synonym for each group of words. Write the word on the line.

forage	immortality	jollity	mete
platoon	rebuttal	squelch	torrent

1. reply, retort, answer _____

2. feed; seek nourishment _____

3. squad, company, outfit _____

4. eternal life, enduring celebrity _____

5. crush, suppress, silence _____

6. glee, gaiety _____

7. downpour, drenching, deluge _____

8. allot, hand out, dispense _____

Part 2 Replace the underlined word with a word from the box that means the same or almost the same. Write your answer on the line.

affect	dimensions	disposal	endear
vertical	novelty	benign	

9. Emily is responsible for the <u>removal</u> of waste paper. _____

10. The new student managed to <u>charm</u> us with his playful antics.

_____

11. Did you measure the <u>proportions</u> of the old barn? _____

12. We set the box down in an <u>upright</u> position. _____

13. Great amounts of stress can <u>influence</u> your health. _____

14. After a while, the <u>newness</u> wore off. _____

15. I'm sure she intended it as a <u>harmless</u> remark, so don't take offense.

_____

ANTONYMS

Antonyms are words that have opposite or nearly opposite meanings.

Part 1 Choose the word from the box that is the best antonym for each group of words. Write the word on the line.

dehydration	falter	harness	immortality	novelty

1. to let run wild _____

2. soaking, flooding, irrigation _____

3. something commonplace or everyday _____

4. death, total obscurity _____

5. go forward, stand strong; unsteady sound _____

Part 2 Replace the underlined word with a word from the box that means the opposite or almost the opposite. Write your answer on the line.

jollity	squelch	jollity	benign	endear

6. They don't like to <u>promote</u> that kind of behavior. _____

7. We dismissed a number of <u>harmful</u> suggestions. _____

8. Her little jokes <u>annoy</u> everyone in the family. _____

9. Her <u>misery</u> rubbed off on all of us. _____

10. The sound of the gong marked the <u>completion</u> of the games.

_____

WORD STUDY

Root Words Choose the word from the box that best completes each of the following sentences.

> prospect   expect   inspect
>
> respect   spectacle   spectator

1. Every _____ cheered as the Olympic runner crossed the finish line.

2. I did not _____ such a warm welcome today.

3. You must _____ her wish to remain nameless.

4. The detective will carefully _____ the scene of the crime.

5. The crowd gathered as the clown made a _____ of herself.

6. Troy was hopeful about the _____ of a long vacation.

Vocabulary in Action

Can you think of a time when you were involved in a disagreement with a friend or family member? What was the most **divisive** issue you've had to contend with? How did it turn out? Were you able to persuade people to compromise?

Before he died on June 29, 1852, Henry Clay was famous for getting people, and even entire states, to compromise. Clay was born on a farm in Virginia in 1777. He became a U.S. representative, a senator, and the Secretary of State during the early 1800s, when tensions between the North and South threatened to split the Union. Henry Clay became known as "the Great Compromiser" when his skills maintained a balance between the free and the slave states. Clay helped draft three pieces of legislation that postponed the Civil War, including The Missouri Compromise and The Compromise of 1850.

In his famous speech on February 6, 1850, Clay argued for the preservation of the Union. Clay said, "I implore, as the best blessing which heaven can bestow upon me upon earth, that if the direful and sad event of the dissolution of the Union shall happen, I may not survive to behold the sad and heart-rending spectacle." His plea was granted when he died in 1852, nine years before the start of the Civil War.

CHALLENGE WORDS

Word Learning—Challenge!

Study the spelling, part of speech, and meaning(s) of each word. Complete each sentence by writing the word on the line. Then read the sentence.

1. **berate** *(v.)* to scold in a harsh way

   I know she'll _____ me for arriving late again.

2. **divisive** *(adj.)* 1. disruptive; 2. causing disagreement or division

   This is a _____ issue, so I prefer not to discuss it.

3. **lucrative** *(adj.)* producing wealth; profitable

   Jody always has some _____ scheme in mind.

4. **meticulous** *(adj.)* 1. very careful about details; 2. fussy

   Christopher is extremely _____ about his homework.

5. **pugnacious** *(adj.)* eager to fight; combative

   A _____ little bulldog lives in that yard.

Use Your Vocabulary—Challenge!

Project Care It's 1943. Jack and Gert know a number of soldiers in the war and decide to raise money to send care packages to all of the soldiers from their town. Write a story about their efforts to organize the people in the town for the fundraiser. Use the five Challenge Words above.

> ### Vocabulary in Action
>
> You can enjoy wordplay and expand your vocabulary by choosing a word and then making a list of all the words that can be made from it. In the Word Study box, you might choose the word *expect* and try to see how many variations of *expect* you can create:
>
> Expect—expected, unexpected, unexpectedly, expecting, expectably, expectedness, expectant, expectancies, expectantly, expectations
>
> Now choose a word from the Word Study box and see how many variations you can create. If you want to challenge yourself further, use each word in a sentence and identify its part of speech.

FUN WITH WORDS

Read the first pair of words on each line and think about the relationship between them. Write a word from the Word List in each blank to create a similar relationship between the second pair of words.

1. **herd** is to **cattle** as _____ is to **soldiers**

2. **daylight** is to **dark** as **duplicate** is to _____

3. **snow** is to **blizzard** as **rain** is to _____

4. **upward** is to **downward** as **horizontal** is to _____

5. **busy** is to **occupied** as **response** is to _____

6. **registration** is to **enrollment** as **graduation** is to _____

7. **build** is to **fire** as _____ is to **portions**

8. **practical** is to **impractical** as **mortality** is to _____

9. **aunt** is to **relative** as **height** is to _____

10. **peace** is to **war** as _____ is to **despair**

Vocabulary in Action

The word *novelty* first appeared in English around 1382. It comes from the Old French word *novelté* ("newness") and the word *novel* ("new, strange, unusual"). The idea of a novelty as an object that is useless but amusing dates to around 1901. The phrase *novelty shop* first appeared around 1973.

CHAPTER 8

WORD LIST

Read each word using the pronunciation key.

afflicted (ə flik´ tid)
bilk (bilk)
commend (kə mend´)
delicacy (del´ ə kə sē)
diminutive (di min´ yə tiv)
dissect (dī sekt´)
endeavor (en dev´ ər)
famine (fam´ in)
frail (frāl)
hectic (hek´ tik)
inadequate (in a´ də kwət)
kindle (kin´ dəl)
minimum (min´ ə məm)
obsolete (ob sə lēt´)
plausible (plô´ zə bəl)
receptacle (re cep´ tə kəl)
scrutinize (skrō̄o´ tə nīz)
stake (stāk)
torrid (tôr´ id)
vestige (ves´ tij)

WORD STUDY

Analogies

Analogies show relationships between pairs of words. Study the relationships between the pairs of words below.

rich is to **poor** as **tall** is to **short**

teacher is to **student** as **doctor** is to **patient**

heat is to **summer** as **cold** is to **winter**

Challenge Words

bellicose (bel´ i kōs)
incorrigible (in côr´ i jə bəl)
matriarch (mā´ trē ärk)
sagacious (sə gā´ shəs)
vilify (vil´ ə fī)

WORDS IN CONTEXT

Read each sentence below to figure out the meaning of the word in **bold**. Use reasoning skills and the remainder of the sentence to help you. Write the meaning of the word on the line.

1. With the popularity of computers, typewriters have become **obsolete**.

   _____

2. My grandmother is **afflicted** with arthritis, but she still likes to paint and to garden.

   _____

3. Jake's **hectic** band schedule includes four performances in a row.

   _____

4. If 30 hours is the maximum, what is the **minimum** number of hours you can volunteer each week?

   _____

5. People rushed to California in 1849 to **stake** a claim and pan for gold.

   _____

6. The **frail** branches of the young tree did not fare well in the windstorm.

   _____

7. Due to the auditorium's inadequate **seating**, some of us had to stand.

   _____

8. The storybook character Thumbelina was able to sleep in a teacup because of her **diminutive** size.

   _____

9. Some people consider cooked flowers a **delicacy**.

   _____

10. We'd better start to **kindle** the fire now because it may take a while.

    _____

Chapter 8   Level H

WORD MEANINGS

Word Learning

Study the spelling, part(s) of speech, and meaning(s) of each word. Complete each sentence by writing the word on the line. Then read the sentence.

1. **afflicted** *(adj.)* 1. suffering with; 2. troubled by

   My cousin is _____ with the flu.

2. **bilk** *(v.)* 1. to cheat out of money; 2. to defraud; 3. to elude

   The police caught the man before he could _____ his creditors out of several thousand dollars.

3. **commend** *(v.)* 1. to praise; 2. to call attention to; 3. to recommend

   I _____ your efforts to improve the situation.

4. **delicacy** *(n.)* 1. fragility; 2. softness; 3. something pleasing to the senses

   She admired the antique lace for its _____.

5. **diminutive** *(adj.)* very small

   She wore a _____ pocket watch on a chain.

6. **dissect** *(v.)* 1. to cut apart or separate; 2. to examine

   I can't wait to _____ worms in biology class!

7. **endeavor** *(n.)* a good try or attempt; *(v.)* to try or strive

   To build your own log cabin is an ambitious _____.
   And now, we will _____ to study for the final exam.

8. **famine** *(n.)* 1. a serious shortage of food; 2. starvation

   My ancestors came here from Ireland during the potato _____.

9. **frail** *(adj.)* 1. not strong or hearty; weak; 2. easily broken

   Mrs. Rulas was _____ after a major operation.

10. **hectic** *(adj.)* marked by feverish activity; hasty

    It's been a _____ day, and we're very tired.

11. **inadequate** *(adj.)* 1. not enough; insufficient; 2. not able

    His _____ efforts to fix the faucet resulted in a huge flood.

12. **kindle** *(v.)* 1. to start a fire; 2. to set in action; 3. to inspire

To our alarm, we saw lightning _____ a fire in the backyard.

13. **minimum** *(n.)* the smallest amount possible; *(adj.)* the least possible

We need a _____ of four dollars.

What is the _____ skill level among the gymnasts on your team?

14. **obsolete** *(adj.)* 1. no longer in use; 2. out-of-date

That garage doesn't sell any _____ auto parts.

15. **plausible** *(adj.)* 1. likely; 2. acceptable; 3. apparently believable

His explanation seems _____ to me.

16. **receptacle** *(n.)* something that holds or contains; a container

Will you throw those apple cores in the trash _____?

17. **scrutinize** *(v.)* 1. to watch carefully; 2. to examine

I will be sure to _____ these papers before I sign them.

18. **stake** *(n.)* a sharpened wood or metal piece hammered into the ground as a marker or support; *(v.)* 1. to indicate boundaries with a stake; 2. to assert a right or an ownership to something

Tie the bottom of the tent to this _____.

Anyone can come and _____ out a territory.

19. **torrid** *(adj.)* 1. dried by the sun's heat; 2. burning

Camels are well adapted to walking on the desert's _____ sands.

20. **vestige** *(n.)* a mark or trace of something no longer present

Mary searched the house for some _____ of the previous owners.

Notable Quotes

"I say in speeches that a **plausible** mission of artists is to make people appreciate being alive at least a little bit. I am then asked if I know of any artists who pulled that off. I reply, 'The Beatles did.'"

—Kurt Vonnegut (1922–2007), author (from *Timequake*)

Chapter 8   Level H

Use Your Vocabulary

Choose the word from the Word List that best completes each sentence. Write the word on the line. You may use the plural form of nouns and the past tense of verbs if necessary.

When my parents were younger, they joined an organization of volunteers who __1__ to assist people in developing countries. My parents went to a country in Africa that was suffering from drought and __2__ . They went to a village where the crops were __3__ with insects.

    At first, the villagers did not trust my parents and feared that the strangers had come to __4__ them out of what little they had. They __5__ my parents' behavior for several weeks before they would listen to their ideas. Finally, Abraha, the leader of the village, sat down to talk with my parents. He found their ideas __6__ , but said they needed to learn more about the plants, animals, and soil in this environment.

    My parents were accustomed to a(n) __7__ pace of life, but the villagers did things more slowly. Abraha showed them __8__ , green plants growing out of the soil. At this stage, they were still healthy, but their __9__ made them vulnerable to insects. The __10__ creatures presented a great threat. Abraha and my mother __11__ seeds to examine them for insects, while my father helped the farmers __12__ out the __13__ fields.

    The village had suffered __14__ rainfall for several years and had nearly __15__ farming equipment— __16__ of long ago. But they did very well with the tools that they had and built large __17__ called cisterns to collect and store the rain that did fall. They hoped that they would get at least the __18__ amount of necessary rain.

    At harvest time, everyone realized that their work had paid off and that luck had provided them with sufficient rain as well. The crops had yielded enough food to eat, and there would even be enough to sell to others. They __19__ one another for their hard work. The successful cooperation __20__ a friendship that my parents and the villagers maintain today.

1. _____

2. _____

3. _____

4. _____

5. _____

6. _____

7. _____

8. _____

9. _____

10. _____

11. _____

12. _____

13. _____

14. _____

15. _____

16. _____

17. _____

18. _____

19. _____

20. _____

SYNONYMS

Synonyms are words that have the same or nearly the same meanings.

Part 1 Choose the word from the box that is the best synonym for each group of words. Write the word on the line.

scrutinize	bilk	commend	inadequate
diminutive	obsolete	afflicted	torrid

1. tiny, miniature, little _____

2. plagued, burdened with _____

3. scorching, parched _____

4. swindle, con, deceive _____

5. compliment, extol, support _____

6. deficient, lacking, incomplete _____

7. defunct, bygone, extinct _____

8. study, consider, ponder _____

Part 2 Replace the underlined word with a word from the box that means the same or almost the same. Write your answer on the line.

kindle	plausible	hectic	receptacle
vestige	frail	endeavor	

9. There's a <u>bucket</u> for the leftover rags in the corner. _____

10. The week continued at a <u>frenzied</u> pace. _____

11. The calligraphy exhibit might <u>arouse</u> your interest. _____

12. She offered no <u>convincing</u> argument for spending so much money.

_____

13. After such a noble <u>effort</u>, I think you will succeed. _____

14. That old hitching post is a <u>remnant</u> of the horse-and-buggy days.

_____

15. I'm afraid the bird will break its <u>fragile</u> bones if it flies into the window.

_____

 **ANTONYMS**

Antonyms are words that have opposite or nearly opposite meanings.

Part 1 Choose the word from the box that is the best antonym for each group of words. Write the word on the line.

afflicted	**commend**	**diminutive**
hectic	**torrid**	**plausible**

1. enormous, gigantic, massive _____

2. slow paced; relaxed _____

3. blame, disapprove, protest _____

4. comfortable, healthy, at ease _____

5. doubtful, questionable, improbable _____

6. frosty, freezing, icy _____

Part 2 Replace the underlined word with a word from the box that means the opposite or almost the opposite. Write your answer on the line.

famine	**inadequate**	**frail**
obsolete	**kindle**	**minimum**

7. Katie set the stereo at the <u>maximum</u> volume level. _____

8. He made a few <u>powerful</u> attempts to move the boulder, but it wouldn't budge.

_____

9. My aunt always tried to <u>smother</u> my interest in theater. _____

10. After the war, the country enjoyed a time of <u>abundance</u>. _____

11. The company has a warehouse full of <u>modern</u> equipment. _____

12. We have <u>sufficient</u> room to move around. _____

WORD STUDY

Analogies To complete the following analogies, decide what kind of relationship is shown by the first pair of words. Then fill in the bubble next to the other pair of words that shows the same relationship.

1. **expose** is to **secret** as
   - **a.** unwrap is to gift
   - **b.** shovel is to snow
   - **c.** write is to table
   - **d.** eat is to food

2. **drizzle** is to **rain** as
   - **a.** remember is to tell
   - **b.** giggle is to snicker
   - **c.** nibble is to eat
   - **d.** hate is to love

3. **caboose** is to **train** as
   - **a.** hat is to hair
   - **b.** dog is to house
   - **c.** glass is to water
   - **d.** suffix is to word

4. **accountant** is to **spreadsheets** as
   - **a.** teacher is to student
   - **b.** barber is to scissors
   - **c.** firefighter is to fire
   - **d.** president is to people

5. **moderate** is to **extreme** as
   - **a.** soft is to loud
   - **b.** blue is to proud
   - **c.** rainy is to cloudy
   - **d.** popular is to lovely

6. **portrait** is to **painting** as
   - **a.** clay is to pot
   - **b.** pen is to pencil
   - **c.** monument is to sculpture
   - **d.** carrot is to garden

CHALLENGE WORDS

Word Learning—Challenge!

Study the spelling, part of speech, and meaning of each word. Complete each sentence by writing the word on the line. Then read the sentence.

1. **bellicose** *(adj.)* eager to start wars or quarrels

   We have as little contact as possible with that _____ group next door.

2. **incorrigible** *(adj.)* unmanageable or unable to be improved

   I won't babysit for them because their little girl is _____.

3. **matriarch** *(n.)* a female who dominates a family or group

   I've never seen a _____ like my Aunt Margaret.

4. **sagacious** *(adj.)* having good judgment or keen perception

   Josh relied on the _____ advice of his older brother.

5. **vilify** *(v.)* to make rude or vicious statements against

   The journalist made up false reports to _____ the city council members.

Use Your Vocabulary—Challenge!

Summer Daze It's a dry summer in your community, and no one's garden is growing. Neighbors are starting to fight over the use of water. On a separate sheet of paper, use the Challenge Words above to write a story about the water shortage and what people do about it. Be creative!

> *Vocabulary in Action*
>
> The word **matriarch** is a combination of two Latin roots. It contains the root *matr*, which means "mother," and *arch*, which means "chief." When you combine these two roots, you arrive at the definition of matriarch, a female who dominates a family or group, in other words, a chief mother.

Twelve vocabulary words are hidden in the puzzle below. Find each word and circle it. Words may be forward, backward, up, down, or diagonal.

```
A M I N T R E V Y L A N F P X I
R F A T H I A Q R H E C T A R S
T I F S T A M U M I N I M R E C
O B S L E R I A A C Y T I G Q R
E A R O I B N K M O V E C T E U
K I N O N C X M E M Q U A C L T
A L L R E R T D I M I N V E M I
T R U C W A N E B E N D E S L N
S T A R J N O L D N I H M S K I
F B R H B I L I J D T X Q I Y Z
R U T I N N X C K A I L N D R E
A T L R Y I R A E R K D T J O K
I K O S T Z K C L P L T I G E R
L A H B R C A Y P E T R O B S O
O Y T A L E L B I S U A L P I B
T O R R I D S T J A G U Q T E R
```

Vocabulary in Action

Before the word **bilk** meant "to defraud," it was a term from the game of cribbage. In cribbage, a bilk happens when a player stops an opponent by spoiling his score. Though no one knows for sure where the word comes from, some scholars believe it is from an Arab word that means "a word signifying nothing." Others think it may be a variation on the word *balk*.

WORD LIST

Read each word using the pronunciation key.

affinity (ə fin´ ə tē)
blanch (blanch)
component (kəm pō´ nənt)
descend (di send´)
diplomat (dip´ lə mat)
diverse (də vərs´)
endorse (en dôrs´)
fantasy (fan´ tə sē)
frequency (frē´ kwən sē)
hedge (hej)
incise (in sīz´)
knoll (nōl)
monarchy (mon´ är kē)
opaque (ō pāk´)
plunder (plun´ dər)
recess (rē´ ses)
secrete (sə krēt´)
stammer (stam´ ər)
tranquil (traŋ´ kwəl)
voluble (vol´ yə bəl)

WORD STUDY

Suffixes

The suffix -*less* means "without, not able to," or "not able to be."

countless (kount´ ləs) *(adj.)* unable to be counted

helpless (help´ ləs) *(adj.)* without help; not able to help oneself

hopeless (hōp´ ləs) *(adj.)* without hope

sleepless (slēp´ ləs) *(adj.)* without sleep; unable to sleep

stainless (stān´ ləs) *(adj.)* without stains; unable to be stained

worthless (wərth´ ləs) *(adj.)* without worth or value

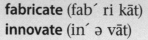

Challenge Words

fabricate (fab´ ri kāt)
innovate (in´ ə vāt)
retrospect (re´ trə spekt)
supplant (sə plant´)
tenacious (tə nā´ shəs)

WORDS IN CONTEXT

Read each sentence below to figure out the meaning of the word in **bold**. Use reasoning skills and the remainder of the sentence to help you. Write the meaning of the word on the line.

1. Always the **diplomat**, Irene calmed her brothers and settled their argument.

   _____

2. Judge Harris told the jury to take a 15-minute **recess**.

   _____

3. The mayoral candidate hoped that the city newspaper would **endorse** him.

   _____

4. After Ben threw the water balloon, I chased him over the **hedge**.

   _____

5. I need boiling water to **blanch** the vegetables before adding them to the sauce.

   _____

6. Tiffany seems to have a natural **affinity** for baseball.

   _____

7. What are the chemical **components** of water?

   _____

8. Ryan was engrossed in a conversation with our **voluble** neighbor.

   _____

9. The noisy children quickly disturbed the park's **tranquil** atmosphere.

   _____

10. We didn't want anyone to see into the garage, so we covered the windows with an **opaque** layer of paint.

   _____

WORD MEANINGS

Word Learning

Study the spelling, part(s) of speech, and meaning(s) of each word. Complete each sentence by writing the word on the line. Then read the sentence.

1. **affinity** *(n.)* a natural liking for or an attraction to someone or something

   The two have a real _____ for each other.

2. **blanch** *(v.)* 1. to take the color from; 2. to whiten; 3. to boil briefly

   I'm afraid the sun will _____ these curtains if we let them hang out to dry.

3. **component** *(n.)* a part; element; ingredient

   Sunlight is a critical _____ of photosynthesis.

4. **descend** *(v.)* to move from a higher place to a lower place

   We sat on the beach at dusk and watched the sun _____ and seem to melt into the horizon.

5. **diplomat** *(n.)* 1. one who represents a government in dealing with other governments; 2. someone skilled in talking effectively with people

   If you want to become a _____, you should learn at least one foreign language.

6. **diverse** *(adj.)* 1. different; 2. having variety

   The United Nations represents many _____ cultures.

7. **endorse** *(v.)* 1. to write one's name on a document to show approval; 2. to approve

   I wanted to do my homework in front of the TV, but my father did not _____ the idea.

8. **fantasy** *(n.)* 1. imagination; a product of the mind; 2. a foolish notion

   She traveled to Hollywood and fulfilled her _____ of becoming an actress.

9. **frequency** *(n.)* 1. how often something happens; 2. number of repetitions of an electrical current

   The _____ of thunderstorms always increases in summer.

10. **hedge** *(n.)* a row of bushes; *(v.)* 1. to confine; 2. to avoid

    Don't _____ the question by trying to divert my attention.

11. **incise** *(v.)* to cut into

    She decided to _____ her initials into the bench.

12. **knoll** *(n.)* a rounded hill or mound

    The coyote stood on the grassy _____ and howled at the rising moon.

13. **monarchy** *(n.)* a government under one leader, such as a king, a queen, or an emperor, usually determined by birth

    The French revolutionaries fought for an end to the _____.

14. **opaque** *(adj.)* unable to be penetrated by light

    An _____ shade hangs in front of the window.

15. **plunder** *(v.)* to rob by open force, as in war; *(n.)* 1. robbery by open force; 2. anything taken by robbery

    During the war, soldiers would _____ small villages.

    Afterwards, they were forced by treaty to return their _____.

16. **recess** *(n.)* 1. a pause in an activity; 2. a small hollow

    We spoke briefly during the _____.

17. **secrete** *(v.)* 1. to give off fluids or other cells from a living body; 2. to hide something away in secret

    Animals recognize other animals by oils and scents that they

    _____.

18. **stammer** *(v.)* to make involuntary interruptions in speech

    She tried not to _____ during her oral report.

19. **tranquil** *(adj.)* 1. free from problems; 2. calm; 3. still

    My old friends live in a _____ village in the mountains.

20. **voluble** *(adj.)* speaking with a steady flow of words; talkative

    With my _____ companion, I couldn't get a word in edgewise.

Vocabulary in Action

The word *fantasy* first appeared in English around 1325 and comes from the Latin *phantasia*, meaning "appearance, image, perception, imagination." People first began to think of a fantasy as a "daydream based on desires" around 1926.

Use Your Vocabulary

Choose the word from the Word List that best completes each sentence. Write the word on the line. You may use the plural form of nouns and the past tense of verbs if necessary.

Maggie lived in a house in the __1__ of a hill. She liked living in the __2__ wilderness, but __3__ the hill into town with some __4__ . Every week she would stand on the grassy __5__ , look down at the town, and say, "Littleville, here I come!"

Everyone in Littleville knew it when Maggie came to visit. She was quite __6__ , and she had a(n) __7__ for foreign languages. Littleville lay on the border of Biggaly and Middley. Many Biggalians and Middlers came to Littleville to live. Maggie enjoyed practicing her languages with the town's __8__ inhabitants. Littleville's Queen Isabel disliked all Biggalians. She felt they wanted to overthrow her __9__ .

One day Maggie arrived in Littleville to find a commotion in the town square. She asked her friend Ivan what was going on.

"Oh, it's terrible," Ivan said. "That horrible mob from Biggaly broke into Judge Lucas's cellar and stole his jewels! The thieves have been captured, but it seems they have __10__ away their __11__ ."

Maggie looked confused. "How did they know his jewels were there? He has __12__ windows and a thorny __13__ around his house. There are several __14__ to this story that I don't understand."

Before Ivan could answer, Queen Isabel stood in front of Lucas's house and called for quiet. Matthias, the Biggalian __15__ , stepped forward.

"Isabel," said Matthias, "I cannot __16__ the arrest of my fellow Biggalians. They did not steal Lucas's jewels."

"That's pure __17__ !" Isabel said. "You know they did. " She turned around, and a thorn from the hedge __18__ a hole in the cloth bag she wore at her belt. Jewels tumbled from the sack.

"Those are my jewels!" Lucas cried. "Isabel, you stole them!" Isabel's face __19__ , and she __20__ , "I—I—I can explain!" But the police came to arrest her before she had the chance.

1. _____

2. _____

3. _____

4. _____

5. _____

6. _____

7. _____

8. _____

9. _____

10. _____

11. _____

12. _____

13. _____

14. _____

15. _____

16. _____

17. _____

18. _____

19. _____

20. _____

SYNONYMS

Synonyms are words that have the same or nearly the same meanings.

Part 1 Choose the word from the box that is the best synonym for each group of words. Write the word on the line.

affinity	component	endorse	opaque
plunder	recess	secrete	voluble

1. subscribe to, support, ratify   _____

2. fondness for, appeal   _____

3. chatty, long-winded   _____

4. loot, ransack; spoils   _____

5. piece, segment, factor   _____

6. issue, discharge, conceal   _____

7. not transparent, obscure   _____

8. break, pause, niche   _____

Part 2 Replace the underlined word(s) with a word from the box that means the same or almost the same. Write your answer on the line.

descend	diverse	fantasy	hedge
knoll	stammer	tranquil	

9. Lacy sat on the <u>hill</u> in the backyard and watched the clouds.

_____

10. Sue sat down to enjoy the <u>peaceful</u> afternoon. _____

11. In awe, we watched the princess <u>come down</u> the staircase. _____

12. If you go into that bakery, you will find a <u>varied</u> assortment of cakes, cookies, and breads. _____

13. When asked to respond to the charges, he could only <u>stutter</u> his reply.

_____

14. Why does he keep trying to dodge the issue? _____

15. Dara was surprised when her mother told her that the tales of the Easter Bunny are all make-believe. _____

 **ANTONYMS**

Antonyms are words that have opposite or nearly opposite meanings.

Part 1 Choose the word from the box that is the best antonym for each group of words. Write the word on the line.

fantasy	blanch	affinity	frequency	diverse

1. rejection, aversion, dislike _____

2. identical, alike, same _____

3. reality, actuality, truth _____

4. rarity, uncommonness _____

5. dye, brighten _____

Part 2 Replace the underlined word with a word from the box that means the opposite or almost the opposite. Write your answer on the line.

descends	endorses	opaque	tranquil	voluble

6. Did you talk to that quiet woman in the blue hat? _____

7. I looked into her troubled face. _____

8. Each morning the spider ascends the doorway and crawls into her web.

_____

9. He wore a clear green stone pinned to his cape. _____

10. Nick disputes the idea, but he is too shy to speak up. _____

WORD STUDY

Suffixes Choose the adjective that best describes each of the following people, objects, or events.

> countless   hopeless   helpless
>
> sleepless   stainless   worthless

1. a newborn baby   _____

2. a long night   _____

3. blades of grass   _____

4. a steel pan   _____

5. a piece of junk   _____

6. a situation   _____

Vocabulary in Action

Are you interested in science and scientific experiments? Maybe you could be the next Elwood Haynes. You may not have heard of Haynes, but you may be familiar with some of his inventions: **stainless** steel, the thermostat, and the horseless carriage. Born in Portland, Indiana, on October 14, 1857, Haynes invented one of the first successful gasoline-powered automobiles. He also invented the thermostat used in houses and many other items. As a young boy, Haynes was curious about how things worked. When he was 12 he read his sister's college chemistry book, and by 15 he was experimenting with metallic substances made of two or more elements. In 1886, natural gas was found in Haynes's hometown. After this discovery, he organized a company to supply it to the town.

CHALLENGE WORDS

Word Learning—Challenge!

Study the spelling, part of speech, and meaning(s) of each word. Complete each sentence by writing the word on the line. Then read the sentence.

1. **fabricate** *(v.)* 1. to make up; 2. to invent

   If you ask him and he doesn't know, he'll _____an answer.

2. **innovate** *(v.)* to develop a new way of doing something

   Necessity often forces people to _____.

3. **retrospect** *(n.)* the act of thinking about the past or looking back

   In _____, I'd say we could have done things differently.

4. **supplant** *(v.)* to take the place of, especially through force or trickery

   The knight thought about his scheme to _____ the monarch.

5. **tenacious** *(adj.)* 1. holding firmly or tightly; 2. persistent or stubborn

   You can try to change her mind, but she is really _____.

Use Your Vocabulary—Challenge!

The Plot Thickens You have discovered a plot to overturn the government of Middley, which is near Littleville and Biggaly. Use the five Challenge Words above to write a story about the schemers and their plans. Are they successful? You decide!

> ### *Vocabulary in Action*
>
> "The memory should be specially taxed in youth, since it is then that it is strongest and most **tenacious.** But in choosing the things that should be committed to memory, the utmost care and forethought must be exercised; as lessons well-learned in youth are never forgotten."
>
> —Arthur Schopenhauer (1788–1860), German philosopher

FUN WITH WORDS

Start your own story notebook. On the lines below, make a list of story ideas. Use at least 10 chapter vocabulary words from this chapter in your list.

Review 7–9

Word Meanings Fill in the bubble of the word that is best defined by each phrase.

1. a fast flow of water
   (a.) famine   (b.) knoll   (c.) torrent   (d.) vestige

2. scorching or fiery
   (a.) torrid   (b.) savory   (c.) diminutive   (d.) opaque

3. not the same
   (a.) benign   (b.) tranquil   (c.) obsolete   (d.) diverse

4. to speak in a halting manner
   (a.) stammer   (b.) plunder   (c.) secrete   (d.) blanch

5. happening at a frantic pace
   (a.) tranquil   (b.) hectic   (c.) vertical   (d.) inadequate

6. one piece of something
   (a.) rebuttal   (b.) novelty   (c.) component   (d.) fantasy

7. seemingly possible or believable
   (a.) afflicted   (b.) voluble   (c.) frail   (d.) plausible

8. to measure out
   (a.) mete   (b.) kindle   (c.) harness   (d.) descend

9. to study with care
   (a.) falter   (b.) scrutinize   (c.) incise   (d.) stake

10. to point out as deserving of praise
   (a.) squelch   (b.) hedge   (c.) commend   (d.) endear

11. to swindle or trick
   (a.) incise   (b.) dissect   (c.) bilk   (d.) stammer

12. to show support for or acceptance of
   (a.) endorse   (b.) mete   (c.) falter   (d.) forage

13. a good effort
   (a.) dehydration   (b.) immortality   (c.) endeavor   (d.) frequency

14. a fondness for someone or something
   (a.) recess   (b.) affinity   (c.) dimension   (d.) receptacle

15. a person who is a skilled negotiator
   (a.) platoon   (b.) diplomat   (c.) monarchy   (d.) commencement

16. a state of merriment
   (a.) jollity   (b.) torrent   (c.) minimum   (d.) component

17. not allowing light to pass through
    a. opaque   **b.** vertical   **c.** torrid   **d.** hectic

18. showing kindness
    a. frail   **b.** voluble   **c.** benign   **d.** plausible

19. anything stolen
    a. knoll   **b.** plunder   **c.** disposal   **d.** novelty

20. to move downward
    a. affect   **b.** endear   **c.** scrutinize   **d.** descend

Sentence Completion
Choose the word from the box that best completes each of the following sentences. Write the word in the blank.

fantasy	platoon	secrete	dehydration	obsolete
dimensions	savory	rebuttal	inadequate	commencement

1. We had a(n) _____ meal at that famous restaurant.

2. Todd gave us _____ directions, but we still made it.

3. Do you know the _____ of your new room?

4. My sister's _____ is stationed overseas.

5. Digital music has made records nearly _____.

6. At one time, the idea of space travel was nothing more than a(n)

_____.

7. June 1 marks the _____ of our summer vacation.

8. The thief decided to _____ the stolen silver, but before he had a chance to do, it he was caught.

9. Take plenty of water on your hike to protect against _____.

10. Each debater has three minutes for _____.

Fill in the Blanks
Fill in the bubble of the pair of words that best completes each sentence.

1. Our teacher said that to _____ a frog, you must _____ its chest cavity.
    a. endorse, harness   **c.** commend, scrutinize
    b. dissect, incise   **d.** blanch, falter

2. Each pirate tried to _____ the others out of their share of the _____.
- **a.** hedge, jollity
- **b.** mete, receptacle
- **c.** bilk, plunder
- **d.** squelch, vestige

3. The tiny pony wears a(n) _____ _____ in the show ring.
- **a.** savory delicacy
- **b.** diminutive harness
- **c.** opaque receptacle
- **d.** frail stake

4. The students will _____ to work with the _____ computers until the new ones arrive.
- **a.** endorse, inadequate
- **b.** descend, hectic
- **c.** endeavor, obsolete
- **d.** falter, afflicted

5. An important _____ gave the _____ speech.
- **a.** dimension, plausible
- **b.** diplomat, commencement
- **c.** platoon, rebuttal
- **d.** delicacy, tranquil

6. When the _____ meal was finished, there was not one _____ of food left over.
- **a.** torrid, torrent
- **b.** vertical, famine
- **c.** hectic, disposal
- **d.** savory, vestige

7. My best friend and I share a(n) _____ for books about the British _____.
- **a.** affinity, monarchy
- **b.** receptacle, dimension
- **c.** immortality, torrent
- **d.** commencement, famine

8. The _____ child _____ himself to his uncle by saying "I love you" over and over again.
- **a.** diverse, kindled
- **b.** tranquil, descended
- **c.** voluble, endeared
- **d.** plausible, commended

9. Dean has a recurring _____ about being the leader of a military _____.
- **a.** component, dehydration
- **b.** rebuttal, stake
- **c.** minimum, monarchy
- **d.** fantasy, platoon

10. A _____ of water rushed down the almost _____ face of the cliff.
- **a.** dehydration, afflicted
- **b.** torrent, vertical
- **c.** recess, tranquil
- **d.** vestige, frail

Classifying Words

Sort the words in the box by writing each word to complete a phrase in the correct category.

benign	blanched	commencement	components	delicacy
diminutive	diplomat	diverse	endeavor	forage
frail	inadequate	immortality	jollity	monarchy
platoon	plausible	recess	savory	scrutinize

Words You Might Use to Talk About Food

1. likes raw vegetables better than _____ ones
2. looking forward to a(n) _____ dessert
3. several _____ of a good meal
4. consider fish eggs a rare _____
5. not have to _____ for food

Words You Might Use to Talk About How People Look

6. pale little boy who is thin and _____
7. an expression of _____ in her twinkling eyes
8. a tall friend and another friend who is _____
9. _____ us with those piercing blue eyes
10. a _____ smile on her friendly face

Words You Might Use to Talk About Careers

11. to join a(n) _____ of soldiers
12. _____ grades for becoming a doctor
13. exciting career as a(n) _____ in the foreign service
14. need to be born to a career in a(n) _____
15. great painters who have achieved _____

Words You Might Use to Talk About Education

16. strange that your school career ends with _____
17. spending time with your friends during _____
18. _____ to learn as much as you can
19. thinking of a(n) _____ excuse for forgetting your homework
20. a _____ range of classes in high school and college

 **WORD LIST**

 WORD STUDY

Read each word using the pronunciation key.

agitate (aj´ ə tāt)
bounteous (boun´ tē əs)
comprise (kəm prīz´)
despondent (di spän´ dənt)
disassociate (dis ə sō´ sē āt)
dominant (däm´ ə nənt)
engaged (in gājd´)
fatigue (fə tēg´)
fugitive (fyoo´ jə tiv)
hesitant (hez´ ə tənt)
indifferent (in dif´ rənt)
laborious (lə bôr´ ē əs)
monopoly (mə näp´ ə lē)
optical (äp´ ti kəl)
portray (pôr trā´)
recluse (rek´ loos)
sedate (si dāt´)
static (stat´ ik)
transact (tran zakt´)
wane (wān)

Root Words

The Greek root *log* means "the study of" or "word."

dialogue (dī´ ə lôg) *(n.)* a conversation; an exchange of ideas
eulogy (yoo´ lə gē) *(n.)* an oral or a written tribute to a person who has died
logistics (lō jis´ tiks) *(n.)* the planning and managing of an undertaking
monologue (mon´ ə lôg) *(n.)* a long speech by one person
technology (tek nol´ ə jē) *(n.)* use of scientific knowledge to solve problems and control physical forces
zoology (zoo lə´ jē) *(n.)* the study of animals

Challenge Words
arbitrary (är´ bə trâr ē)
conspicuous (kən spik´ yoo əs)
envisage (en vis´ əj)
lackadaisical (lak ə dāz´ i kəl)
optimum (op tə´ məm)

WORDS IN CONTEXT

Read each sentence below to figure out the meaning of the word in **bold**. Use reasoning skills and the remainder of the sentence to help you. Write the meaning of the word on the line.

1. You won't get any suggestions from her; she's **indifferent** on the matter.

   _____

2. When cold weather comes, my interest in swimming tends to **wane**.

   _____

3. A washing machine **agitates** clothes in soapy water to clean them.

   _____

4. Josh was **engaged** in a discussion with a customer, so we didn't bother him.

   _____

5. According to legend, an old **recluse** has lived in that cave for 50 years.

   _____

6. Beth will **portray** Helen Keller in our school production of *The Miracle Worker*.

   _____

7. Javier appeared **hesitant** to join the soccer team, but he decided to in the end.

   _____

8. Who has the **dominant** influence in this group?

   _____

9. Our **bounteous** garden produced flowers of all sizes and colors.

   _____

10. I always hear too much **static** on my portable radio.

    _____

WORD MEANINGS

Word Learning

Study the spelling, part(s) of speech, and meaning(s) of each word. Complete each sentence by writing the word on the line. Then read the sentence.

1. **agitate** *(v.)* 1. to shake or stir; 2. to upset or excite emotionally

    I didn't want to _____ the situation, so I said nothing.

2. **bounteous** *(adj.)* 1. giving generously; 2. ample or plentiful

    We sat down to a _____ feast.

3. **comprise** *(v.)* 1. to include or contain; 2. to make up

    This is one of the four verses that _____ the song.

4. **despondent** *(adj.)* 1. feeling sad or discouraged; 2. wanting to give up

    Jessie lost her job, so she's feeling rather _____.

5. **disassociate** *(v.)* to end contact with someone or something

    I think that after all this trouble, she'll probably _____ herself from that group.

6. **dominant** *(adj.)* 1. ruling or controlling; 2. foremost

    Over there you can see the _____ wolf in the pack.

7. **engaged** *(adj.)* 1. busy or occupied; 2. planning to be married

    Can Harry come with us on Friday, or is he otherwise _____?

8. **fatigue** *(n.)* 1. weariness; 2. mental or physical exhaustion; *(v.)* to tire out

    He went to the doctor complaining of _____ and headaches.

    Reading without sufficient light will _____ your eyes.

9. **fugitive** *(adj.)* running away or escaping; *(n.)* someone who is running away from the law

    We have finally captured the _____ chicken thief.

    The police are searching for a dangerous _____.

10. **hesitant** *(adj.)* 1. holding back; 2. not able to decide

    Why are you so _____ to jump in the pool?

11. **indifferent** *(adj.)* 1. having no interest in; 2. having no feeling about or opinion of

    She was _____ to his pleas and cries for mercy, and she grounded him.

12. **laborious** *(adj.)* requiring or involving hard work or effort

    The group worked for two weeks with _____ intensity.

13. **monopoly** *(n.)* complete control of a business or service by one group

    That company used to have a _____ , but now there are several different telephone companies.

14. **optical** *(adj.)* of or having to do with eyes and eyesight

    McKinley decided to have an _____ exam.

15. **portray** *(v.)* 1. to make a picture of; 2. to describe in words; 3. to act out onstage

    The inspector tried to _____ the situation in a positive light.

16. **recluse** *(n.)* someone who lives apart from others; *(adj.)* apart from others; solitary

    After the accident, Joe turned into a _____.

    Sometimes I dream of a _____ existence in the mountains.

17. **sedate** *(adj.)* calm; settled; composed

    This is a fairly _____ crowd compared to last year's.

18. **static** *(adj.)* 1. having no motion; 2. at rest; *(n.)* 1. atmospheric electricity; 2. interference with radio or TV reception due to electric disturbance; 3. strong opposition

    You can't ask a baby to hold a _____ pose for that long.

    We couldn't hear the radio program because of all the _____.

19. **transact** *(v.)* to do, to carry out, or to perform business

    The officers have met to _____ a business deal.

20. **wane** *(v.)* to gradually decrease in size or amount; *(n.)* a gradual decrease or lessening

    The fox's interest in the squirrel began to _____.

    Tonight the moon is on the _____.

Use Your Vocabulary

Choose the word from the Word List that best completes each sentence. Write the word on the line. You may use the plural form of nouns and the past tense of verbs if necessary.

Last summer, I chose to compete with Alex, the __1__ kid on the block. I didn't try to beat him at basketball, but at business. I interfered with his __2__ on the neighborhood lawn-mowing market.

The idea came to me one hot day. My buddy Tyler and I were sitting on the porch, __3__ because we had no money. Just then, Alex walked by and stapled a flyer to a telephone pole. According to his flyer, his business is __4__ of mowing lawns, trimming hedges, and weeding gardens. The sign __5__ my melting brain.

"That's it!" I said. "We can mow lawns too." Tyler just shrugged and looked __6__.

"Come on, Ty," I persisted. "We could have a(n) __7__ summer. Think of the cash we could make!"

"I don't know." He sounded __8__. "Mowing lawns in the hot sun sounds awfully __9__. Besides, who'll hire us? Alex does all the yards around here."

"Ty," I said. "A few lawns a week won't __10__ you. And I know where to start. Alex doesn't work for Mr. Maloney." Tyler, normally very __11__, jumped away from me and looked nervous.

"There's no way I'm going near that house!"

Mr. Maloney lives in an old, peeling house on the corner. He's been a(n) __12__ for 20 years. The kids all __13__ him as a deformed and dangerous __14__ hiding from the FBI. I could see Tyler's interest in earning money begin to __15__. He __16__ himself from the entire project, so I went down to the corner by myself.

I knocked on his door and waited. The entire house remained __17__. Finally, the door opened. For a moment, I could only stare. Was this a(n) __18__ illusion? I saw before me a smiling, grey-haired man.

"I'm sorry I took so long," Mr. Maloney said. "I was __19__ on the phone. How can I help you?" I told him I'd come to __20__ a business deal. He invited me in for lemonade, and he became the first of my many customers that summer.

1. _____
2. _____
3. _____
4. _____
5. _____
6. _____
7. _____
8. _____
9. _____
10. _____
11. _____
12. _____
13. _____
14. _____
15. _____
16. _____
17. _____
18. _____
19. _____
20. _____

SYNONYMS

Synonyms are words that have the same or nearly the same meanings.

Part 1 Choose the word from the box that is the best synonym for each group of words. Write the word on the line.

comprise	despondent	dominant	fugitive
hesitant	indifferent	transact	wane

1. reluctant, unsure, faltering   _____

2. fleeing; runaway, outlaw   _____

3. diminish, fade; decline   _____

4. governing, prevailing, primary   _____

5. depressed, melancholy, hopeless   _____

6. consist of, include   _____

7. nonchalant, unconcerned, detached   _____

8. conduct, negotiate, deal   _____

Part 2 Replace the underlined word with a word from the box that means the same or almost the same. Write your answer on the line.

agitate	engaged	fatigue	static
portray	optical	recluse	

9. In his story, Jude chose to <u>depict</u> the man as a wretched villain.

    _____

10. My cousin is <u>betrothed</u> to a movie star. _____

11. Zach is having <u>visual</u> problems lately. _____

12. Don't <u>disturb</u> the baby, or he'll never go back to sleep. _____

13. Our neighbor is turning into a <u>hermit</u>; we haven't seen her in weeks.

    _____

14. The circles under her eyes showed her <u>exhaustion</u>. _____

15. We are hoping to spend a <u>quiet</u> evening at home. _____

 **ANTONYMS**

Antonyms are words that have opposite or nearly opposite meanings.

Part 1 Choose the word from the box that is the best antonym for each group of words. Write the word on the line.

agitate	comprise	despondent	sedate	wane

1. exclude, lack   _____

2. upset, ruffled, frantic   _____

3. still, quiet, calm   _____

4. lighthearted, happy, elated   _____

5. enlarge, grow; increase   _____

Part 2 Replace the underlined word with a word from the box that means the opposite or almost the opposite. Write your answer on the line.

laborious	engaged	fatigue	indifferent	hesitant

6. Anne is the most <u>involved</u> member of the team. _____

7. The clown's <u>liveliness</u> is contagious. _____

8. Are you <u>available</u> on Friday afternoon? _____

9. We noticed his extremely <u>confident</u> manner right away. _____

10. It's really an <u>effortless</u> task. _____

WORD STUDY

Root Words Write the word from the box that has most to do with each described profession.

> dialogue   eulogy   logistics
>
> monologue   technology   zoology

1. one who works to protect endangered animals _____

2. a preacher, especially at a funeral _____

3. a writer of novels or short stories _____

4. a computer engineer _____

5. a person who plans all the details of a big wedding _____

6. a comedian _____

Vocabulary in Action

In order to stretch your word knowledge, look at each word in the Word Study box and identify its part of speech. Then try to figure out what you need to do to make the word function as a different part of speech. For example, the word *dialogue* is most often a noun, occasionally a verb. If you change the word to *dialogic*, you create an adjective.

CHALLENGE WORDS

Word Learning—Challenge!

Study the spelling, part of speech, and meaning(s) of each word. Complete each sentence by writing the word on the line. Then read the sentence.

1. **arbitrary** *(adj.)* 1. existing or occurring by chance; 2. based on one's own judgment, without restriction

    You can't just make _____ changes to the rules.

2. **conspicuous** *(adj.)* attracting attention by being unusual

    Please don't make any _____ noises during the concert.

3. **envisage** *(v.)* to imagine or visualize

    How do you _____ your future?

4. **lackadaisical** *(adj.)* showing little or no interest or energy

    Peggy's _____ approach to her schoolwork frustrated her teachers.

5. **optimum** *(n.)* something that is most favorable; *(adj.)* best or most favorable

    Among film ratings, four stars is the _____.

    This critic rarely gives a film the _____ rating.

Use Your Vocabulary—Challenge!

Summer Job Description It's summertime! You have been wanting to earn extra money, and you've found your dream job for the summer. Write a story about your job, using the five Challenge Words above.

> ### Vocabulary in Action
>
> Because English is a living language, more words are being added to it all the time. Some slang expressions you know today might someday be the source of a legitimate word.
>
> This is the origin of the whimsical word *lackadaisical*, which first appeared in English around 1768. It comes from the interjection *lackadaisy*, "alas, alack," and is an alteration of *lack-a-day* (1695). One who cried "lack-a-day" was considered sentimental.

Write an advertisement for a summer business you'd like to start. Tell people what you can do for them and why they should hire you. Use at least 10 vocabulary words from this chapter in your ad.

WORD LIST

Read each word using the pronunciation key.

agonize (ag´ ə nīz)
bravado (brə vä´ dō)
confer (kən fər´)
detention (di ten´ shən)
discipline (dis´ ə plən)
drone (drōn)
engineer (en jə nēr´)
feat (fēt)
fundamental (fun də men´ təl)
hoard (hôrd)
infinite (in´ fə nit)
lament (lə ment´)
multitude (mul´ tə tood)
optimistic (op tə mis´ tik)
pragmatic (prag mat´ ik)
recourse (rē´ kôrs)
sequence (sē´ kwəns)
stimulate (stim´ yə lāt)
transit (tran´ zit)
weary (wēr´ ē)

WORD STUDY

Prefixes

The prefix *mis-* means "bad, badly," or "wrongly."

misanthrope (mis´ ən thrōp) *(n.)* one who does not trust people
misbehave (mis bi hāv´) *(v.)* to behave badly
misfortune (mis fôr´ chən) *(n.)* bad luck
misspell (mis spel´) *(v.)* to spell incorrectly
mistake (mis stāk´) *(v.)* to wrongly identify; *(n.)* an error
misunderstand (mis un dər stand´) *(v.)* to not understand or comprehend

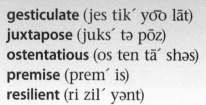

Challenge Words

gesticulate (jes tik´ yoo lāt)
juxtapose (juks´ tə pōz)
ostentatious (os ten tā´ shəs)
premise (prem´ is)
resilient (ri zil´ yənt)

WORDS IN CONTEXT

Read each sentence below to figure out the meaning of the word in **bold**. Use reasoning skills and the remainder of the sentence to help you. Write the meaning of the word on the line.

1. When the **weary** traveler finally made it home, she collapsed into bed.

   _____

2. I mailed your letter last week; it must still be in **transit**.

   _____

3. The committee will meet to **confer** about the proposed changes to the lunchroom policy.

   _____

4. To teach your dog **discipline**, begin training while it's a puppy.

   _____

5. The band played in Central Park before a **multitude** of fans.

   _____

6. The tightrope walker enthralled the crowd with his skill and **bravado**.

   _____

7. The **drone** visited several flowers and then flew back to the hive.

   _____

8. The appearance of Cass's story in the magazine was quite a **feat** for her.

   _____

9. Lada kept a **hoard** of DVDs she wouldn't let us use.

   _____

10. My only **recourse** was to take the broken MP3 player to the store manager.

   _____

WORD MEANINGS

Word Learning

Study the spelling, part(s) of speech, and meaning(s) of each word. Complete each sentence by writing the word on the line. Then read the sentence.

1. **agonize** *(v.)* 1. to suffer great physical or emotional pain; 2. to make a major effort

   You don't have to _____ over this decision.

2. **bravado** *(n.)* a showy display of courage or bravery

   Underneath his _____, I think he's nervous.

3. **confer** *(v.)* 1. to discuss together; 2. to share ideas

   Why don't you _____ with your teacher about your grade?

4. **detention** *(n.)* 1. the act of delaying or keeping behind; 2. the condition of being held behind

   Mr. Jeffreys chose to enforce the _____ of students after class.

5. **discipline** *(n.)* 1. training to learn or improve; 2. behavior that follows rules of conduct; *(v.)* 1. to drill or train by instruction; 2. to punish

   I think Sari has the _____ required to become a great dancer.

   The captain really knows how to _____ her troops.

6. **drone** *(v.)* to make a constant dull humming sound; *(n.)* 1. a dull humming sound; 2. a male bee

   I can hear the engines _____ from here.

   I couldn't sleep because of the _____ of a car alarm outside.

7. **engineer** *(n.)* 1. a person who designs or builds an operating system; 2. one who operates an engine; *(v.)* to plan, build, or manage

   We will need an _____ to design and build the new bridge.

   Here is the fellow who will _____ the new playground.

8. **feat** *(n.)* an act of hard work, strength, or great accomplishment

   The acrobat prepared for several months for the performance of her crowning _____ on the trapeze.

9. **fundamental** *(adj.)* of a foundation or basis; basic; *(n.)* an essential or important part

    The vote of the people is _____ to a democracy.

    The relationship between a subject and verb is a _____ of grammar.

10. **hoard** *(n.)* a hidden supply of something stored for future use; *(v.)* to gather by saving or hiding

    I'll have to reach into my _____ of chocolate bars.

    Squirrels begin to _____ nuts and seeds long before winter begins.

11. **infinite** *(adj.)* having no boundaries or limit; endless

    My uncle seems to have an _____ supply of stories to tell.

12. **lament** *(n.)* a song or poem of grief; *(v.)* 1. to feel or show grief; 2. to regret deeply

    Mara sang a bitter _____ of a lost love.

    We all _____ the loss of our good friend.

13. **multitude** *(n.)* a great, indefinite number

    Vicky gazed up into the _____ of stars.

14. **optimistic** *(adj.)* likely to expect the best result or outcome

    I am not too _____ about finishing on time.

15. **pragmatic** *(adj.)* having a practical point of view

    Jim is no dreamer; he always gives very _____ suggestions.

16. **recourse** *(n.)* an instance of turning to someone or something for help

    My only _____ was to ask the librarian for help.

17. **sequence** *(n.)* 1. the following of one thing after another; 2. a particular order

    We must perform the tasks in their correct _____.

18. **stimulate** *(v.)* to move or rouse to action

    TV does not _____ your mind the way a book does.

19. **transit** *(n.)* passage over, across, or through

    The package was lost in _____ somewhere.

20. **weary** *(adj.)* tired; having fatigue

    I am _____ of all this arguing.

Use Your Vocabulary

Choose the word from the Word List that best completes each sentence. Write the word on the line. You may use the plural form of nouns and the past tense of verbs if necessary.

I went sailing for the first time last week, which was no small **1** for me. I've always been afraid of boats. When Teri and her brother asked me if I would join them, I smiled and said with **2** , "Oh, I love to sail," although I was secretly terrified. For a week I **3** over my decision. How could I back out of the situation? I **4** with my friend Sarah, who told me to go. Ever **5** , she told me I'd have a great time breathing in the sea air. I am more **6** , however, and I just wanted to avoid seasickness.

The day of the sail I woke up early and began to panic. What if something went wrong? A(n) **7** of possible catastrophes ran through my head. What if it rained? What if the boat capsized? I filled my backpack with a towel and dry clothes. I also packed my **8** of dimes and quarters—just in case I needed money. I kept thinking of the **9** possibilities for disaster. How could I cancel? I could tell them later that I'd had to serve a Saturday **10** . But I knew that I had no **11** , and **12** with worry, I left the house to meet Teri and her brother.

I rode my bike to the dock, using all my self-**13** . Teri showed me how to climb onto the boat, and before I knew it, we were under way. I began to **14** the loss of solid ground under my feet. Teri noticed my white knuckles gripping the edge of the seat. "Don't worry," she said. "This boat is **15** for safety, and my brother is a great sailor."

Gradually, I relaxed my grip as I watched the other two perform the **16** of steps necessary to raise the sails. Soon we were in smooth **17** across the lake. I listened to the peaceful, faraway **18** of an airplane. I really began to enjoy myself!

When we docked the boat, I said to Teri, "Well, you've **19** my interest. Do you think your brother could teach me the **20** of sailing?"

1. _____

2. _____

3. _____

4. _____

5. _____

6. _____

7. _____

8. _____

9. _____

10. _____

11. _____

12. _____

13. _____

14. _____

15. _____

16. _____

17. _____

18. _____

19. _____

20. _____

SYNONYMS

Synonyms are words that have the same or nearly the same meanings.

Part 1 Choose the word from the box that is the best synonym for each group of words. Write the word on the line.

detention	bravado	agonize	engineer
lament	stimulate	recourse	pragmatic

1. struggle, endure   _____

2. mourn, sorrow   _____

3. heroics, swaggering, blustering   _____

4. constraint, confinement   _____

5. planner, builder; design   _____

6. rational, logical, reasonable   _____

7. appeal, resource, refuge   _____

8. excite, incite, agitate   _____

Part 2 Replace the underlined word(s) with a word from the box that means the same or almost the same. Write your answer on the line.

hoard	transit	feat	infinite
confer	sequence	weary	

9. My sisters and I will <u>consult</u> about what to buy for Mom's birthday.

_____

10. Jake can always dip into his <u>stash</u> of money. _____

11. He seems to have an <u>endless</u> supply of excuses. _____

12. We are all proud of your great academic <u>achievement</u>. _____

13. Can we rehearse the scenes in the <u>right order</u>? _____

14. The <u>worn-out</u> horse fell asleep at the stable door. _____

15. She is terribly busy visiting people; she's always in <u>motion</u>. _____

ANTONYMS

Antonyms are words that have opposite or nearly opposite meanings.

Part 1 Choose the word from the box that is the best antonym for each group of words. Write the word on the line.

> stimulate   bravado   agonize   drone   infinite

1. enjoy, celebrate, relax _____

2. finite, definite, measurable _____

3. deaden, paralyze, stun _____

4. shriek; high-pitched sound _____

5. cowardice, fear, modesty _____

Part 2 Replace the underlined word with a word from the box that means the opposite or almost the opposite. Write your answer on the line.

> multitude   lament   pragmatic   optimistic   weary

6. When we heard that our neighbors were leaving, we began to <u>rejoice</u>.

_____

7. If you want gadgets, we have a <u>few</u>. _____

8. George has a very <u>idealistic</u> approach to solving problems. _____

9. It's a real challenge to work with such an <u>energetic</u> group. _____

10. No matter where we are, my father always has a <u>pessimistic</u> outlook.

_____

> ### Vocabulary in Action
>
> Most cities in the United States were built around the automobile. In many places, public transportation, or mass *transit,* is not available. Even large cities often lack reliable public transportation. One exception is New York City, the only city in America where more than half the people do not own an automobile. About 33 percent of the nation's mass transportation riders live in or near New York City. Other major U.S. cities that boast solid public transit systems are Boston, Chicago, San Francisco, and Washington, D.C.

WORD STUDY

Prefixes Choose the word from the box that best completes each of the following sentences.

> misanthrope   misbehave   misunderstand
>
> misfortune   misspell   mistake

1. Raffaella hates it when people _____ her name.

2. Matt promised not to _____ while his parents were away.

3. Don't be surprised if she makes nasty comments; she's a real

   _____.

4. Try not to _____ one twin for the other.

5. Speak clearly so I don't _____ what you are saying.

6. As I watched our empty boat float away, I could not believe our

   _____.

> ## Vocabulary in Action
>
> Philosophy, literature, art, and music are full of
> ***misanthropes***. In literature, one of the most famous
> misanthropes is Moliére's character Alceste, the
> protagonist of the 1666 play *The Misanthrope*.
>
> In the play, Alceste rejects his culture's polite social
> conventions. This makes him extremely unpopular.
> Alceste sums up his attitude with the statement
> "Mankind has grown so base, I mean to break with
> the whole human race." However, his determination
> to reject society is countered by his desire to share a
> life with the lovely Célimène, whose actions oppose
> all he stands for.

CHALLENGE WORDS

Word Learning—Challenge!

Study the spelling, part of speech, and meaning(s) of each word. Complete each sentence by writing the word on the line. Then read the sentence.

1. **gesticulate** *(v.)* to create motions with the hands to show feeling or add force to what one is saying

   When the mayor speaks publicly, she _____ and speaks with authority.

2. **juxtapose** *(v.)* to place close together or side by side

   For contrast, she chose to _____ pictures of Texas and Alaska.

3. **ostentatious** *(adj.)* done for show; intended to attract attention

   I am tired of her _____ displays of wealth.

4. **premise** *(n.)* an assumption that is taken for granted but not proved

   We are working on the _____ that the show won't start on time.

5. **resilient** *(adj.)* having the ability to recover or adjust to change

   Always _____, he dried his tears and started over.

Use Your Vocabulary—Challenge!

A Sailor's Story Lucia Lemon is a champion sailor who has sailed around the world several times. She is the best sailor there is, and she knows it. Her archrival, Gwen Grape, has challenged her to a race. Use the five Challenge Words above to write a story about the race between Lucia and Gwen.

> ### *Vocabulary in Action*
>
> In logic, a ***premise*** (ca. 1374) is a "previous proposition from which another follows." It comes from the Middle Latin word *premissa*—"the proposition set before."

FUN WITH WORDS

Each of the following names has a vocabulary word from this chapter hidden in it. Underline the chapter words in the names.

1. Mag O'Nizer

2. B. R. Avadon

3. Fred Rone

4. Ben G. Ineerson

5. Mare Coursen

6. K. W. Eary

7. Louise Quencen

8. Chad I. Sciplinee

9. Misti Mulatec

10. Lin F. Initer

Now make up your own names with the following vocabulary words hidden in them.

11. detention _____

12. transit _____

13. pragmatic _____

14. feat _____

15. lament _____

16. confer _____

17. fundamental _____

18. hoard _____

19. multitude _____

20. optimistic _____

Notable Quotes

"Some of the world's greatest **feats** were accomplished by people not smart enough to know they were impossible."

—Doug Larson (1902–1981), British middle-distance runner

CHAPTER 12

WORD LIST

Read each word using the pronunciation key.

allocate (al´ ə kāt)
brim (brim)
conform (kən fôrm´)
dethrone (dē thrōn´)
disconnected (dis kə nek´ tid)
dubious (dōō´ bē əs)
entitle (in tīt´ əl)
ferocious (fə rō´ shəs)
furlough (fər´ lō)
horizontal (hôr ə zän´ təl)
inkling (iŋk´ liŋ)
laud (lôd)
murmur (mər´ mər)
ordeal (ôr dēl´)
precise (pri sīs´)
rectify (rek´ tə fī)
shirk (shərk)
stoic (stō´ ik)
tumult (tōō´ mult)
wrath (rath)

WORD STUDY

Suffixes

The suffix *-ment* means "the act or state of" or "means of."

amazement (a māz´ mənt) *(n.)* the state of being amazed

commitment (kə mit´ mənt) *(n.)* the act of committing or pledging to do something in the future

employment (em ploi´ mənt) *(n.)* the state of being employed

monument (mon´ yə mənt) *(n.)* a memorial erected as a means of remembering a person or an event

ornament (ôr´ nə mənt) *(n.)* an object or a feature used as decoration

payment (pā´ mənt) *(n.)* the act of paying

Challenge Words

affirmation (af ər mā´ shən)
auspicious (ô spi´ shəs)
demeanor (di mēn´ ər)
enormity (e nôr´ mə tē)
prerogative (pri räg´ ə tiv)

Read each sentence below to figure out the meaning of the word in **bold**. Use reasoning skills and the remainder of the sentence to help you. Write the meaning of the word on the line.

1. We stood on the **brim** of the canyon and looked down into the valley.

   _____

2. The judges will surely **laud** your brilliant attempts to create electricity from water.

   _____

3. The newspaper will **rectify** the error by reprinting the article without the mistakes.

   _____

4. Fearing the **wrath** of the storm, we huddled in the basement.

   _____

5. The club has decided to **allocate** the money to buy decorations for the fall carnival.

   _____

6. If the bottom half of the box doesn't **conform** to the top half, it won't close.

   _____

7. This ticket will **entitle** you to one ride on the roller coaster.

   _____

8. From backstage, the actors could hear the **murmur** of the audience.

   _____

9. Mrs. Merten took **precise** measurements so our uniforms would fit perfectly.

   _____

10. My brother is home from the army on a two-week **furlough**.

   _____

WORD MEANINGS

Word Learning

Study the spelling, part(s) of speech, and meaning(s) of each word. Complete each sentence by writing the word on the line. Then read the sentence.

1. **allocate** *(v.)* to set aside for a special purpose

   The school chose to _____ money for a new gym.

2. **brim** *(n.)* the upper edge of anything hollow

   Don't fill my cup to the _____.

3. **conform** *(v.)* 1. to be or make similar in form; 2. to act in harmony with; to comply

   My brother doesn't like to _____ to anyone else's ideas.

4. **dethrone** *(v.)* to remove from a position of power

   There was a movement to _____ the king.

5. **disconnected** *(adj.)* 1. apart from; 2. not connected

   I _____ my telephone so I could get some sleep.

6. **dubious** *(adj.)* doubtful or full of uncertainty

   She gave me a _____ look and said, "Are you sure about that?"

7. **entitle** *(v.)* 1. to give a particular name or title to; 2. to give a claim or right to; 3. to qualify

   Do you think your ideas _____ you to special treatment?

8. **ferocious** *(adj.)* 1. fierce or savage; 2. extreme or severe

   In the cave, there lived a _____ beast.

9. **furlough** *(n.)* 1. time away; 2. a leave of absence or vacation

   Her supervisors granted her a two-week _____.

10. **horizontal** *(adj.)* parallel to the ground; *(n.)* something that goes across

    The carpenters laid a _____ beam across the hole in the floor.

    Mr. Martinek drew a _____ line across the top of the graph.

11. **inkling** *(n.)* 1. a hint; a slight suggestion; 2. a vague understanding

    I don't have the slightest _____ of what you're talking about.

12. **laud** *(v.)* to praise or glorify

    Hundreds of people came to _____ the new king.

131

13. **murmur** *(n.)* a low, unclear, constant sound; *(v.)* to make a low, unclear, constant sound

   From my bedroom, I could hear the _____ of the stream.

   In her sleep, my sister began to _____ something about lunch.

14. **ordeal** *(n.)* a difficult or painful experience

   I don't know how she will survive this _____.

15. **precise** *(adj.)* 1. clearly and carefully stated; 2. distinct; 3. exact

   We gave _____ directions to the park from the school.

16. **rectify** *(v.)* to make right

   How will you _____ the situation?

17. **shirk** *(v.)* to put off work or duty in order to avoid

   I hope you don't _____ your responsibilities while I'm gone.

18. **stoic** *(adj.)* not showing feeling; restrained or impassive

   She wore a _____ expression on her face through the entire funeral.

19. **tumult** *(n.)* 1. a loud disturbance of a large crowd; 2. any confusion of the mind or feelings

   The fight on the soccer field caused a _____ among the crowd.

20. **wrath** *(n.)* violent anger or rage

   Woe to the poor mortal on whom Zeus unleashes his _____!

Vocabulary in Action

How did Pennsylvania get its name? Its founder, English reformer William Penn, named it in honor of his father.

Persecuted in England for refusing to renounce his Quaker faith and *conform* to the rules of the Anglican church, Penn came to America in 1682 and established Pennsylvania as a place where people could practice religion freely. The colony became a haven for minority religious sects from Germany, Holland, Scandinavia, and Great Britain.

In a 1682 document, Penn guaranteed absolute freedom of worship in Pennsylvania. Rich in fertile lands as well as religious freedom, the colony attracted settlers and grew rapidly. Thanks to William Penn, Pennsylvania, which guaranteed religious freedom for its citizens, was established in the New World.

Use Your Vocabulary

Choose the word from the Word List that best completes each sentence. Write the word on the line. You may use the plural form of nouns and the past tense of verbs if necessary.

In social studies class, we **1** the achievements of women in history. Our teacher felt that we were too **2** from the past and wanted to give us at least a(n) **3** of the women who have contributed to our world. Each student reached over the **4** of a bowl and pulled out the name of a famous woman. Then we had to write a short report. We responded at first with **5** of discontent, but once we got started, we were really interested by the women and some of the **6** they survived.

Many of these women chose not to **7** to the typical expectations. Deborah Sampson Gannett dressed as a man and fought with **8** bravery in the Revolutionary War. Another warrior, Ladshmi Bai, led Indian troops to fight those who wanted to **9** the king of the small kingdom of Jhansi.

Although no blood may be shed, political battles can become **10** as well. Elizabeth Cady Stanton caused a(n) **11** in the late 1800s by declaring to a(n) **12** public that women should be **13** to vote. She and her friend Susan B. Anthony **14** much of their time in the attempt to **15** this injustice. They inspired the **16** of many men and conservative women, but in 1920, the 19th Amendment to the Constitution let women vote.

Women have made contributions to science and the arts as well. Polish physicist Marie Curie's **17** scientific research led to the discovery of two elements—polonium and radium. Painter Georgia O'Keeffe used her paintings to capture the **18** lines and distinct colors of the New Mexico landscape.

Many women have worked in politics. Congresswoman Shirley Chisholm took an extended **19** from her political career to become a professor, encouraging women to go into politics. When Corazón Aquino's husband was killed, she did not **20** her duty. She became the next president of the Philippines.

1. _____

2. _____

3. _____

4. _____

5. _____

6. _____

7. _____

8. _____

9. _____

10. _____

11. _____

12. _____

13. _____

14. _____

15. _____

16. _____

17. _____

18. _____

19. _____

20. _____

SYNONYMS

Synonyms are words that have the same or nearly the same meanings.

Part 1 Choose the word from the box that is the best synonym for each group of words. Write the word on the line.

conform	laud	entitle	disconnected
ordeal	precise	rectify	wrath

1. frenzy, rage, fury _____

2. difficulty, strain, trial _____

3. definite, well-defined, accurate _____

4. correct, improve, repair _____

5. agree, match, modify _____

6. detached, separated, distant _____

7. label, allow, permit _____

8. compliment, applaud, extol _____

Part 2 Replace the underlined word with a word from the box that means the same or almost the same. Write your answer on the line.

allocate	brim	dubious	ferocious
inkling	shirk	tumult	

9. I came home with a <u>wild</u> hunger. _____

10. I have a <u>suspicion</u> that she's never been here before. _____

11. Due to the <u>suspicious</u> nature of the man's complaints, the judge dismissed the case. _____

12. Mark's confession has caused quite a <u>stir</u>. _____

13. I chipped my tooth on the <u>rim</u> of the mug. _____

14. Every year we <u>earmark</u> part of our budget for entertainment.

_____

15. At the beginning of summer vacation, he began to <u>neglect</u> his chores at home.

_____

ANTONYMS

Antonyms are words that have opposite or nearly opposite meanings.

Part 1 Choose the word from the box that is the best antonym for each group of words. Write the word on the line.

> conform   entitle   dubious   stoic   disconnected

1. deprive, disallow   _____

2. certain, sure, positive   _____

3. emotional, feeling, indulgent   _____

4. together, united, joined, connected   _____

5. conflict, differ, disagree   _____

Part 2 Replace the underlined word with a word from the box that means the opposite or almost the opposite. Write your answer on the line.

> ferocious   horizontal   laud   murmur   precise

6. The people will <u>condemn</u> her methods of ruling. _____

7. I stifled a <u>mild</u> desire to shout out loud. _____

8. I heard the mother <u>shout</u> something to her child. _____

9. Everyone noticed his <u>careless</u> movements on the dance floor.

_____

10. Adam set down the ironing board in a <u>vertical</u> position. _____

WORD STUDY

Suffixes Decide which of the words from the box could be used in each sentence to replace the underlined word. Write the word on the line.

amazement	commitment	employment
monument	ornament	payment

1. I couldn't find any <u>work</u> the whole summer. _____

2. Joe made a <u>promise</u> to finish the project. _____

3. To my <u>surprise</u>, everyone had gone home. _____

4. She has put her <u>check</u> in the mail already. _____

5. We have removed every <u>decoration</u> from the tree. _____

6. The <u>statue</u> is visible from miles away. _____

Vocabulary in Action

The Washington **Monument** in Washington, D.C., was completed on December 6, 1884. It is the focal point of the National Mall, as well as the background for concerts and fireworks.

How long did it take to complete the 555-foot Egyptian obelisk, topped with a 3,300-pound marble capstone and a 9-inch pyramid of cast aluminum? That question is harder to answer than it may seem. The Washington National Monument Society laid the monument's cornerstone in 1848 on Independence Day, 36 years before completion. But when the obelisk was at a height of about 156 feet, the society lost support and funding. The monument stood incomplete and untouched for 20 years.

Finally, in 1876, President Ulysses S. Grant authorized the U.S. Army Corps of Engineers to finish the project. When fully constructed, it was the world's tallest structure. Today, the approximately 36,000-stacked blocks of granite and marble compose the world's tallest freestanding masonry structure. The 9-inch aluminum pyramid, which completes the top of the structure as it narrows to a point, is 100 ounces of solid aluminum. Aluminum was a rare metal in the 1880s, selling for $1.10 per ounce. The pyramid was the largest piece of aluminum of its day.

CHALLENGE WORDS

Word Learning—Challenge!

Study the spelling, part(s) of speech, and meaning(s) of each word. Complete each sentence by writing the word on the line. Then read the sentence.

1. **affirmation** *(n.)* confirmation that something is correct

   She looked to her teacher for an _____ of her talents.

2. **auspicious** *(adj.)* showing promise of success or good fortune

   The club introduced its _____ leaders.

3. **demeanor** *(n.)* 1. outward manner; 2. behavior or conduct

   Libby's shy _____ made it hard to get to know her.

4. **enormity** *(n.)* extreme wickedness or atrocious character

   I don't think you understand the _____ of the situation.

5. **prerogative** *(n.)* an exclusive or special right that belongs to a person or group

   If she wants to move to Mexico, that's her _____.

Use Your Vocabulary—Challenge!

Newspaper Article You are a journalist who is attending a city council meeting on the subject of the city parks. There is a group who believes that children should not be allowed to use public athletic fields without a permit. Use the five Challenge Words above to write an article about the meeting.

> ### Vocabulary in Action
>
> The word *auspicious* (ca. 1596) means "of good omen." It comes from the Latin *auspicium*, meaning "divination by observing the flight of birds."

FUN WITH WORDS

Use the clues to complete the puzzle. Choose from the vocabulary words in this chapter.

Across

2. going across
5. a confusion or stir
6. great anger
10. to make match
11. uncertain
13. to put aside for a certain thing
14. to avoid something

Down

1. a low, constant sound
3. to pay a compliment
4. showing no emotion
7. to permit
8. exact
9. time off
11. to remove a leader from power
12. a hard time

Review 10–12

Word Meanings Fill in the bubble of the word that is best defined by each phrase.

1. to move forcefully
   - a. hoard
   - **b. agitate**
   - c. lament
   - d. entitle

2. to make weary or exhaust
   - a. lament
   - b. wane
   - **c. fatigue**
   - d. murmur

3. a remarkable achievement
   - **a. feat**
   - b. tumult
   - c. furlough
   - d. detention

4. without beginning or end
   - a. precise
   - b. dubious
   - c. horizontal
   - **d. infinite**

5. a slight hint or suggestion
   - **a. inkling**
   - b. recluse
   - c. drone
   - d. brim

6. to leave undone what should be done
   - **a. shirk**
   - b. transact
   - c. rectify
   - d. discipline

7. to get smaller, weaker, or dimmer
   - a. stimulate
   - b. entitle
   - **c. wane**
   - d. allocate

8. looking at things in a matter-of-fact way
   - a. bounteous
   - **b. pragmatic**
   - c. sedate
   - d. fundamental

9. to be the same or similar
   - a. comprise
   - **b. conform**
   - c. confer
   - d. disassociate

10. to collect secretly and store away
    - a. dethrone
    - b. laud
    - c. agonize
    - **d. hoard**

11. to play the part of in a play or movie
    - **a. portray**
    - b. sedate
    - c. stimulate
    - d. laud

12. an unpleasant experience
    - a. fugitive
    - **b. ordeal**
    - c. feat
    - d. recourse

13. forced delay or confinement
    - a. recluse
    - b. fatigue
    - **c. detention**
    - d. wrath

14. wild and fierce
    - **a. ferocious**
    - b. optical
    - c. indifferent
    - d. dominant

15. giving more than enough
    - **a. bounteous**
    - b. pragmatic
    - c. weary
    - d. precise

16. to discuss thoughts and ideas
    - a. disassociate
    - **b. confer**
    - c. portray
    - d. transact

© Loyola Press.

17. to mourn or grieve
    (a.) lament   (b.) shirk   (c.) discipline   (d.) rectify

18. not moving or changing
    (a.) despondent   (b.) stoic   (c.) hesitant   (d.) static

19. a steady flow of quiet, unclear sound
    (a.) monopoly   (b.) murmur   (c.) wrath   (d.) fugitive

20. passage through, across, or over
    (a.) drone   (b.) multitude   (c.) transit   (d.) brim

Sentence Completion

Choose the word from the box that best completes each of the following sentences. Write the word in the blank.

optical	rectify	furlough	indifferent	despondent
disconnected	allocates	bravado	engineered	hesitant

1. I was _____ to accept my brother's seemingly innocent offer.

2. The designers _____ the new system to work automatically.

3. Alex spent the day trying to _____ a computer error.

4. Maggie took a(n) _____ from her job and went to Australia for a month.

5. I bought my red-and-white striped glasses at the new _____ shop.

6. Stewart was _____ when we didn't get the part in the play.

7. Pedro put on a good show of _____ in front of the bully, but we knew he was really terrified.

8. The U.S. Congress _____ funds to run the national parks.

9. Although I am physically _____ from my family, we talk daily.

10. Kayla's _____ attitude toward her grades shows in her sloppy work.

Fill in the Blanks

Fill in the bubble of the pair of words that best completes each sentence.

1. As the boring TV show _____ on, my _____ got the best of me, and I fell asleep.
    (a.) agonized, bravado   (c.) engineered, furlough
    (b.) allocated, static   (d.) droned, fatigue

2. A(n) _____ is a person who does everything possible to _____ from other people.
   a. monopoly, dethrone
   c. recluse, disassociate
   b. ordeal, allocate
   d. transit, hoard

3. The group of _____ met to _____ about an exciting new design concept.
   a. engineers, confer
   c. recluses, murmur
   b. inklings, conform
   d. fugitives, agitate

4. Students who _____ their obligations in Mr. Sewell's class will find themselves in _____ in a hurry.
   a. shirk, detention
   c. allocate, furlough
   b. portray, discipline
   d. agonize, tumult

5. It's good to be _____ about the future, but you must be _____ too.
   a. ferocious, hesitant
   c. fundamental, precise
   b. despondent, disconnected
   d. optimistic, pragmatic

6. Andy hoped a show of _____ would make people think he was the _____ player on the team.
   a. discipline, dubious
   c. fatigue, indifferent
   b. bravado, dominant
   d. tumult, fundamental

7. How can anyone who is about to receive a two-week _____ be _____?
   a. ordeal, dubious
   c. furlough, despondent
   b. engineer, indifferent
   d. monopoly, hesitant

8. The winning ticket _____ you to receive a _____ of prizes.
   a. comprises, hoard
   c. conforms, wrath
   b. entitles, multitude
   d. agitates, feat

9. Mom had no _____ but to _____ us for staying out so late.
   a. bravado, comprise
   c. sequence, fatigue
   b. inkling, entitle
   d. recourse, discipline

10. The _____ wolf kept its place as leader by acting _____ around the other wolves in the pack.
    a. dominant, ferocious
    c. hesitant, fatigued
    b. indifferent, agitated
    d. optimistic, despondent

Classifying Words
Sort the words in the box by writing each word to complete a phrase in the correct category.

agitate allocate bounteous bravado conform

despondent discipline dominant drone   entitled

ferocious fugitive hoard   infinite laborious

multitude murmur precise rectify weary

Words You Might Use to Talk About Animal Behavior

1. dangerous to _____ the python's cage

2. _____ animal expecting to eat first

3. tiny dogs displaying lots of _____

4. _____ coyote hiding in the woods

5. the bared teeth of a(n) _____ lion

Words You Might Use to Talk About Engineers

6. each client _____ to personal attention

7. able to take _____ measurements

8. the _____ to spend long hours studying

9. _____ to the client's needs and expectations

10. be able to _____ flaws in the design

Words You Might Use to Talk About Sounds

11. the annoying _____ of a buzzing fly in the window

12. _____ sobs over the broken heirloom

13. the _____ of secretive voices behind a closed door

14. ragged, _____ breathing of the winded runner

15. _____ sigh from the baby's tired sitter

Words You Might Use to Talk About Amounts

16. cheered by the _____ supply of good things to eat

17. hiding a(n) _____ of cookies in the back of a drawer

18. a(n) _____ number of stars on a clear night

19. a field that contains a(n) _____ of flowers

20. to _____ the shares of the profits fairly

WORD LIST

Read each word using the pronunciation key.

amiable (ā´ mē ə bəl)
brisk (brisk)
controversy (kon´ trə vər sē)
detract (di trakt´)
discord (dis´ kôrd)
durable (dŏŏr´ ə bəl)
envelop (en vel´ əp)
fervent (fər´ vənt)
fury (fyŏŏr´ ē)
hostility (ho stil´ i tē)
inquisitive (in kwiz´ ə tiv)
legible (lej´ ə bəl)
mutilate (myŏŏt´ əl āt)
oscillate (os´ ə lāt)
predator (pred´ ə tər)
reiterate (rē it´ ə rāt)
siege (sēj)
subordination (sə bôr də nā´ shən)
twinge (twinj)
wretched (rech´ id)

WORD STUDY

Root Words

The root *man* or *manu* means "hand."

manacle (man´ ə kel) *(n.)* handcuff
manage (man´ ij) *(v.)* to take charge of; to supervise
manicure (man´ i kyŏŏr) *(n.)* a treatment for the care of the hands and fingernails
manipulate (mə nip´ yə lāt) *(v.)* 1. to handle with skill; 2. to skillfully influence, often unfairly
manual (man´ yŏŏ əl) *(adj.)* 1. operated by hand; 2. of or requiring physical human effort
manuscript (man´ yə skript) *(n.)* a text written by hand or computer

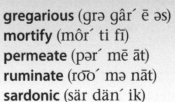

Challenge Words

gregarious (grə gâr´ ē əs)
mortify (môr´ ti fī)
permeate (pər´ mē āt)
ruminate (rŏŏ´ mə nāt)
sardonic (sär dän´ ik)

WORDS IN CONTEXT

Read each sentence below to figure out the meaning of the word in **bold**. Use reasoning skills and the remainder of the sentence to help you. Write the meaning of the word on the line.

1. As they grew older, the jealousy and **discord** between the two sisters gave way to a strong friendship.

   _____

2. The lion is the most powerful **predator** on the plains of Africa.

   _____

3. I want a fan that **oscillates** so we can cool both sides of the room.

   _____

4. If you **mutilate** a library book by ripping its pages, the library will revoke your card.

   _____

5. Our server is busy and overworked; she doesn't deserve this kind of **hostility** from her customers.

   _____

6. Did you hear me the first time, or should I **reiterate** my request?

   _____

7. Pam felt a **twinge** of regret as she saw her brother drive away.

   _____

8. I like to take a **brisk** walk after eating a big meal.

   _____

9. Her handwriting on the card was barely **legible**, so I asked her to read it to me.

   _____

10. In Charles Dickens's novel *Oliver Twist*, the orphans lived in a **wretched** house and ate only gruel and water.

   _____

WORD MEANINGS

Word Learning

Study the spelling, part of speech, and meaning(s) of each word. Complete each sentence by writing the word on the line. Then read the sentence.

1. **amiable** *(adj.)* 1. agreeable and friendly; 2. good-natured

   The United States has an _____ relationship with many countries.

2. **brisk** *(adj.)* lively; quick; active

   She conducted the class at a _____ pace.

3. **controversy** *(n.)* a disagreement or debate between opposing sides

   The newest postage stamps are a subject of great _____.

4. **detract** *(v.)* 1. to lessen; 2. to take away a good part of something

   I hope my absence didn't _____ from all the fun.

5. **discord** *(n.)* 1. a lack of agreement; 2. a harsh noise

   The meeting consisted only of argument and _____; we accomplished nothing.

6. **durable** *(adj.)* 1. lasting; 2. able to withstand wear or weathering

   I need a good, _____ pair of boots for the winter.

7. **envelop** *(v.)* 1. to enclose with a wrap or cover; 2. to surround completely

   We waited for the coming fog to _____ the house.

8. **fervent** *(adj.)* 1. showing great emotion or warmth; 2. ardent; 3. enthusiastic

   His most _____ wish was to meet his favorite basketball player in person.

9. **fury** *(n.)* fierce anger or rage

   After I crashed her car, I could not bear to face her _____.

10. **hostility** *(n.)* 1. unfriendliness; the state of being enemies; 2. opposition to an idea

    The board of directors showed _____ toward our new idea.

11. **inquisitive** *(adj.)* 1. extremely curious; 2. eager to learn

    Wyatt, our pet ferret, is an _____ little fellow and gets into everything.

12. **legible** *(adj.)* 1. easily read; 2. apparent

When you hand in your next paper, please make it more _____.

13. **mutilate** *(v.)* to cut off, tear, or damage an important part of something

My baby sister manages to _____ any delicate thing that she touches.

14. **oscillate** *(v.)* to swing back and forth

I watched with fascination as the dolls in the shop window began to

_____.

15. **predator** *(n.)* 1. an animal that attacks other animals or living things; 2. a person who attacks others

Because the deer have no natural _____ anymore, the population is growing.

16. **reiterate** *(v.)* to say over again; to repeat

Before we finish, I would like to _____ my point about the heavy traffic.

17. **siege** *(n.)* the surrounding of a location for the purpose of capture

The troops have brought the entire city under _____.

18. **subordination** *(n.)* 1. placement in a lower class or rank; 2. obedience

The king insisted upon the complete _____ of the palace staff.

19. **twinge** *(n.)* 1. a sudden, sharp pain; 2. a sudden emotional pain

Every time I move my knee, I feel a _____ of pain.

20. **wretched** *(adj.)* 1. living a miserable life; 2. in very poor condition

The old, _____ house sat alone in the middle of the field.

Use Your Vocabulary

Choose the word from the Word List that best completes each sentence. Write the word on the line. You may use the plural form of nouns and the past tense of verbs if necessary.

I didn't mean to start a(n) **1** , but no one thought I would beat the Kid at his best video game. The Kid, as he is commonly known, is a perfectly nice, **2** person until it comes to video games. Then he becomes a vicious **3** looking for innocent victims to devour. Before I begin, I'd like to **4** that I didn't mean to start anything last Tuesday; it just happened.

It all started with a barely **5** note in my locker. "Be at Tom's after school, or I'll come find you." Tom is our classmate, who regularly invites gamers to play at his home. The note was signed, "the Kid." I knew better than to ignore his tone of **6** . If the Kid had picked me as his next opponent, then I had to show up. And besides, my **7** nature led me to wonder why he had chosen me and how the event would play out. Might I even win? It was my **8** hope that I would not.

Without meaning to **9** from the Kid's reputation as a great player, I'll tell you now that I knew I was better. But I also knew that if I beat the Kid, he would unleash his **10** on me. I did not cherish the idea of a(n) **11** kick in the seat of the pants! Truly, I wanted to avoid all **12** .

I arrived at Tom's place **13** by a group of my buddies. They were to serve as protection in case the Kid decided to try and **14** me. He waited for me in the living room.

"You **15** creature," the Kid said as he eerily **16** in a chair. "I hope you're made of **17** stuff, because I'm gonna' pound you." We walked over to the console, and the game began.

It didn't last long. Within five minutes, I had his troops under **18** . I felt only a(n) **19** of regret as my generals and I demanded his **20** . The Kid looked stunned. He hung his head for a minute and then looked up at me.

"Hey," he said. "What do you say you and me form a team? Together, we could beat everyone in town!"

1. _____
2. _____
3. _____
4. _____
5. _____
6. _____
7. _____
8. _____
9. _____
10. _____
11. _____
12. _____
13. _____
14. _____
15. _____
16. _____
17. _____
18. _____
19. _____
20. _____

SYNONYMS

Synonyms are words that have the same or nearly the same meanings.

Part 1 Choose the word from the box that is the best synonym for each group of words. Write the word on the line.

amiable	detract	fury	legible
controversy	discord	mutilate	twinge

1. cramp, spasm, pang   _____

2. dispute, argument, quarrel   _____

3. deform, mangle, cripple   _____

4. pleasant, social, benevolent   _____

5. ferocity, wrath, ire   _____

6. conflict, clash, disharmony   _____

7. diminish, reduce, subtract   _____

8. plain, clear, understandable   _____

Part 2 Replace the underlined word with a word from the box that means the same or almost the same. Write your answer on the line.

brisk	durable	envelop	fervent
hostility	reiterate	wretched	

9. Her coat used to be so big that it would enwrap her. _____

10. Why do you treat me with such antagonism? _____

11. We stopped at the fence for a quick chat. _____

12. You may ask the teacher to repeat her instructions. _____

13. The president issued an impassioned plea for help. _____

14. The photographs showed masses of forlorn people standing in line.

_____

15. The paint that we put on the house should be lasting. _____

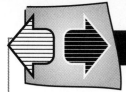

ANTONYMS

Antonyms are words that have opposite or nearly opposite meanings.

Part 1 Choose the word from the box that is the best antonym for each group of words. Write the word on the line.

detract	discord	durable	envelop	legible

1. unwrap, expose, unveil   _____

2. increase, add to, enhance   _____

3. unreadable, unclear, indistinct   _____

4. fragile, flimsy, weak   _____

5. agreement, accord, harmony   _____

Part 2 Replace the underlined word with a word from the box that means the opposite or almost the opposite. Write your answer on the line.

amiable	brisk	fervent	inquisitive	wretched

6. A <u>prosperous</u> young woman lives in that house. _____

7. The new student is most <u>unconcerned</u> about how our school works.

   _____

8. The two countries engaged in a series of <u>hostile</u> negotiations.

   _____

9. We did not expect such a <u>cool</u> response to our invitation. _____

10. Lisa and Sally went for a <u>lazy</u> walk along the river's edge. _____

Vocabulary in Action

The word **amiable** first appeared in English around 1350 and comes from those who spoke Old French. They adapted it from the Latin word *amicabilis*, meaning "friendly." *Amiable* has the same root as the feminine name *Amy*, which means "beloved."

WORD STUDY

Root Words Each of the words in the box originally comes from a related word in Latin. Sometimes it comes from a related word in another language that also has roots in Latin. Read the word histories below. Choose the word from the box that matches each history.

manacle	manicure	manual
manage	manipulate	manuscript

1. Latin *manuale* (something that can be held in the hand) _____

2. Latin *manus* (hand) + Latin *cura* (care) _____

3. French *manicle* (handcuff) _____

4. Italian *maneggiare* (to handle or train, especially horses) _____

5. Latin *manus* (hand) + Latin *scriptus* (written) _____

6. French *manipuler* (to handle an apparatus) _____

Vocabulary in Action

Harry Houdini was a master of illusion. He earned an international reputation as an escape artist who dramatically freed himself from ropes, shackles, and handcuffs, also known as **manacles**. He was married to Wilhelmina Rahner, who, as Beatrice Houdini, was his stage assistant. He performed on vaudeville and appeared in many motion pictures.

Houdini, originally named Erik Weisz, was born in 1874 in Budapest, Hungary. However, he claimed to have been born in Appleton, Wisconsin. Houdini died in Detroit, Michigan, on October 31, 1926.

CHALLENGE WORDS

Word Learning—Challenge!

Study the spelling, part of speech, and meaning(s) of each word. Complete each sentence by writing the word on the line. Then read the sentence.

1. **gregarious** *(adj.)* enjoying the company of others

   My aunt Cathy is more _____ than my father is.

2. **mortify** *(v.)* to cause shame or humility

   My parents _____ me when they tell stories about me as a baby.

3. **permeate** *(v.)* to spread completely throughout

   A bad mood tends to _____ the whole group.

4. **ruminate** *(v.)* 1. to ponder; 2. to think over carefully

   They left me to _____ over the decision I have to make.

5. **sardonic** *(adj.)* sarcastic in a bitter or mocking way

   I did not appreciate her _____ response to my complaint.

Use Your Vocabulary—Challenge!

Twin Trouble Bailey and Jesse are twins, but they are nothing alike. Bailey is very talkative, while Jesse is more on the shy side. As always, they have their birthday party together, but this year they get in an argument in front of their friends. Using the five Challenge Words above, write a story about the party, the argument, and the resolution. Be creative!

> ## Notable Quotes
>
> "Speak to me as to thy thinkings,
> As thou dost **ruminate**, and give thy worst of thoughts
> The worst of words."
>
> —William Shakespeare (1564–1616),
> British playwright (from *Othello*)

In chemistry, letters are used to represent different chemicals and elements. Equations such as the one below show how elements combine to form compounds:

$$2H_2 + O_2 = 2H_2O$$

This shows how hydrogen (H) and oxygen (O) can be combined to make water. In word chemistry, you'll see an equation like the one above. The letters in each equation combine to make a vocabulary word. A small number to the right of a letter tells you how many times that letter appears in the word. The clue next to the equation gives you a hint. For example:

$IS + E_2G$ = keeping you occupied _____

The small 2 tells you there are two *E*'s in this vocabulary word. Determine how many letters are actually in the word. Then rearrange them and write the answer on the line. The answer to the example is *siege*.

1. $LBI + MA_2E$ = a formula for friendliness _____

2. $CAE + T_2DR$ = a solution that lessens _____

3. $CIO + SD_2R$ = this won't agree with you _____

4. $TRF + NE_2V$ = something enthusiastic _____

5. $OPL + NE_2V$ = to enclose something _____

6. $TNE + SUV + I_4Q$ = like people who ask questions _____

7. $R_4ZUY_2F - YR_3Z$ = this may make you angry _____

8. $EI_3B_2 + KS_2R - EI_2SB$ = an active formula _____

WORD LIST

Read each word using the pronunciation key.

antic (an´ tik)
buoy (boo´ ē)
credible (kred´ ə bəl)
devise (di vīz´)
discriminate (di skrim´ ə nāt)
ecology (ē kol´ ə jē)
esteem (e stēm´)
fiasco (fē as´ kō)
gale (gāl)
humble (hum´ bəl)
integral (in´ tə grəl)
liable (lī´ ə bəl)
mythical (mith´ i kəl)
paragon (pâr´ ə gon)
preliminary (pri lim´ ə nâr ē)
reliability (ri lī ə bil´ i tē)
silhouette (sil ōo et´)
succumb (sə kum´)
tycoon (tī kōon´)
yarn (yärn)

WORD STUDY

Prefixes

The prefix *extra-* means "outside of" or "beyond."

extract (ek strakt´) *(v.)* to pull or draw out, often with special effort
extracurricular (ek strə kə rik´ yə lər) *(adj.)* outside of normal classwork
extradite (ek´ strə dīt) *(v.)* to give up an alleged criminal to another state or authority
extraneous (ek strā´ nē əs) *(adj.)* not relevant
extraordinary (ek strôr´ dən er ē) *(adj.)* out of the ordinary
extravagant (ek strav´ ə gənt) *(adj.)* more than is necessary

Challenge Words

accolade (ak´ ə lād)
desultory (des´ əl tôr ē)
exorbitant (ig zôr´ bi tənt)
novice (näv´ is)
pinnacle (pin´ ə kəl)

© Loyola Press.

153

Level H

Read each sentence below to figure out the meaning of the word in **bold**. Use reasoning skills and the remainder of the sentence to help you. Write the meaning of the word on the line.

1. I have great **esteem** for those who volunteer at the homeless shelter.

_____

2. After the birthday cake fell on the floor, I knew that the party would be a **fiasco**.

_____

3. The **gale** ripped the umbrella from my hands and tore the leaves from the trees.

_____

4. The runners competed in a **preliminary** race before proceeding to the finals.

_____

5. Sue is a **credible** witness; I believe her account of the accident.

_____

6. Dennis is always getting in trouble for some **antic**, such as putting bubble bath in the town fountain.

_____

7. Grandma is in the kitchen telling Nicky a **yarn** about her days in the army.

_____

8. She had decorated the tapestry with giants, dragons, and other **mythical** creatures.

_____

9. If you break the window, you will be **liable** for the cost of replacing it.

_____

10. My Uncle Leon is a well-known **tycoon** in the athletic-shoe industry.

_____

WORD MEANINGS

Word Learning

Study the spelling, part(s) of speech, and meaning(s) of each word. Complete each sentence by writing the word on the line. Then read the sentence.

1. **antic** *(n.)* a foolish act or prank

   What _____ are you up to now?

2. **buoy** *(n.)* a floating device used in water as a marker or warning

   Be sure you don't swim past the _____.

3. **credible** *(adj.)* 1. believable; trustworthy, 2. reliable

   Forgetting your homework is not a _____ excuse.

4. **devise** *(v.)* 1. to plan; 2. to invent

   They will _____ a plan to get him out of the dungeon.

5. **discriminate** *(v.)* 1. to distinguish between; 2. to observe a difference; 3. to show prejudice

   A young child often cannot _____ between a helpful stranger and a dangerous one.

6. **ecology** *(n.)* the study of the relationship between living things and their environment

   If you knew anything about _____, you would not throw your garbage in that stream.

7. **esteem** *(v.)* 1. to think of with respect; 2. to consider valuable; *(n.)* respect or admiration

   We all _____ the judge and her wise decisions.

   I hold my parents in great _____.

8. **fiasco** *(n.)* a complete failure

   If the new cabinet falls apart, we'll have a complete _____ on our hands.

9. **gale** *(n.)* a very strong, powerful wind

   The little straw house could not resist the great _____.

10. **humble** *(adj.)* modest; not overly proud of one's own accomplishments; *(v.)* to humiliate or destroy the pride of

    The _____ princess never tried to promote herself.

    A defeat after so many successes would really _____ him.

11. **integral** *(adj.)* necessary to make a whole

   A goalie is _____ to every soccer team.

12. **liable** *(adj.)* responsible for, according to law

   We are _____ to pay for the damages caused by the accident.

13. **mythical** *(adj.)* 1. having to do with traditional stories about spirits, ancestors, or heroes; 2. imaginary

   Many people have compared John F. Kennedy's presidency to the

   _____ kingdom of Camelot.

14. **paragon** *(n.)* a model of excellence

   My sister is hardly a _____ of virtue.

15. **preliminary** *(adj.)* coming before the main part; introductory; *(n.)* a statement or action that comes before others

   We should start with a _____ discussion of what we plan to do.

   The introduction of the speaker is an important _____.

16. **reliability** *(n.)* dependability; the ability to be counted on

   I am not too sure of the _____ of that car.

17. **silhouette** *(n.)* the outline of something; *(v.)* to show in outline

   I could see the _____ of my mother through the window shade.

   The bright lights _____ his head from behind.

18. **succumb** *(v.)* 1. to give in to a stronger force; 2. to die

   I will not _____ to your wishes!

19. **tycoon** *(n.)* a wealthy or powerful businessperson

   He started as a clerk but grew to be an industry _____.

20. **yarn** *(n.)* 1. a heavy thread used for knitting and weaving; 2. a story of adventure

   I used green and blue _____ for the scarf.

Use Your Vocabulary

Choose the word from the Word List that best completes each sentence. Write the word on the line. You may use the plural form of nouns and the past tense of verbs if necessary.

Last summer, a computer industry __1__ offered to take my Scout troop out on his yacht. Mr. Hartley is very powerful and wealthy, but he has remained __2__ and selfless. He is __3__ throughout the community as a(n) __4__ of generosity.

Mr. Hartley believes that the firsthand exploration of nature is __5__ to every child's development. Our troop had been studying marine __6__, so we were excited to see this mysterious world for ourselves.

Early one sunny Saturday, we all gathered at the dock. Mr. Hartley spoke a few __7__ words of welcome. Then, using maps and a compass, he helped us __8__ our course for the day. He also demonstrated the boat's __9__ by showing us that everything was in top condition. He assigned each scout a different task and didn't __10__ against any one of us. All of our chores were equally demanding. Finally, he warned us against any __11__. Boating was serious business, he said.

By afternoon, the sky had darkened, and a strong __12__ made it difficult to steer the boat. Mr. Hartley knew he was __13__ for our safety, and we were far from the dock. He knew his boat wouldn't __14__ to the storm, but he wanted to get us to a protected area.

He steered the boat toward the mouth of a nearby cove. A bright red __15__ floated at the cove's entrance, warning us of shallow water. But he was a __16__ leader. We had complete confidence in his ability.

The cove protected us from the storm. The area had a(n) __17__ quality about it. I could imagine magical sea creatures hiding in these waters. Mr. Hartley helped us pass the time by making animal-shaped __18__ on the wall in the lantern light. He also told us great __19__ about his adventures at sea. Late in the afternoon, the storm stopped and we headed home. Mr. Hartley apologized for the __20__, but to us, the trip had been a great adventure.

1. _____
2. _____
3. _____
4. _____
5. _____
6. _____
7. _____
8. _____
9. _____
10. _____
11. _____
12. _____
13. _____
14. _____
15. _____
16. _____
17. _____
18. _____
19. _____
20. _____

SYNONYMS

Synonyms are words that have the same or nearly the same meanings.

Part 1 Choose the word from the box that is the best synonym for each group of words. Write the word on the line.

buoy	esteem	gale	liable
credible	fiasco	integral	mythical

1. gust, windstorm _____

2. value, honor; regard, approval _____

3. answerable, accountable, obligated _____

4. legendary, illusory, fabled _____

5. disaster, blunder, washout _____

6. essential, needed _____

7. faithful, plausible, dependable _____

8. marker, beacon, signal _____

Part 2 Replace the underlined word with a word from the box that means the same or almost the same. Write your answer on the line.

tycoon	succumb	antic	paragon
humble	devise	discriminate	

9. That was nothing but a lark. _____

10. We must formulate a method of transporting our products. _____

11. A great building entrepreneur lives in that mansion. _____

12. Whatever you do, don't yield to his charms. _____

13. She went on to college to become a model of scholarship. _____

14. In the museum business, one must be able to distinguish between real and counterfeit paintings. _____

15. Martin cast a modest glance in our direction. _____

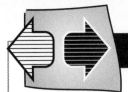

ANTONYMS

Antonyms are words that have opposite or nearly opposite meanings.

Part 1 Choose the word from the box that is the best antonym for each group of words. Write the word on the line.

> humble   liable   mythical   reliability   succumb

1. real, actual, factual _____

2. proud, conceited; praise, glorify _____

3. exempt, unaccountable, not responsible _____

4. resist, fight, survive, live _____

5. unworthiness, instability _____

Part 2 Replace the underlined word with a word from the box that means the opposite or almost the opposite. Write your answer on the line.

> esteem   fiasco   credible   integral   preliminary

6. He presented a great deal of <u>unreliable</u> evidence to the jury. _____

7. I hold artists and musicians in great <u>contempt</u>. _____

8. Our swim team won the <u>final</u> race. _____

9. Yvonne provided us with many ideas <u>unnecessary</u> to the project.

_____

10. The carnival was a great <u>success</u>. _____

Vocabulary in Action

The word **mythical** can be traced to about 1678. Its root is from the Greek *mythos*—"speech, thought, story, myth." According to the *Dictionary of English Folklore*, myths are "stories about divine beings, generally arranged in a coherent system; they are revered as true and sacred; they are endorsed by rulers and priests; and closely linked to religion. Once this link is broken, and the actors in the story are not regarded as gods but as human heroes, giants or fairies, it is no longer a myth but a folktale. Where the central actor is divine but the story is trivial . . . the result is religious legend, not myth." (p. 254)

WORD STUDY

Prefixes Choose the word from the box that best completes each of the following sentences.

> extract   extradite   extraordinary
>
> extracurricular   extraneous   extravagant

1. Her parents could not afford to support her _____ taste in clothing.

2. She may be small, but she possesses _____ strength.

3. Just tell me the basic story; you can leave out _____ details.

4. The United States agreed to _____ the German war criminal.

5. How will you ever _____ yourself from that terrible situation?

6. He keeps very busy with all of his _____ activities.

Vocabulary in Action

Did you know that **extracurricular** activities first made their appearance in American colleges in the 19th century? The first extracurricular activities were student literary societies, or debate clubs. By the middle of the century, Greek fraternities and sororities emerged. Students also initiated and organized the early athletic programs at American colleges.

By the start of the 20th century, literary societies were on the decline, and some educators felt that less desirable extracurricular activities were now distracting students from their curricular responsibilities. Intercollegiate athletics soon became the dominant element in the extracurriculum in most American colleges and high schools. Such activities as school newspapers and interschool sports programs have been part of American high schools since the World War I era.

CHALLENGE WORDS

Word Learning—Challenge!

Study the spelling, part of speech, and meaning(s) of each word. Complete each sentence by writing the word on the line. Then read the sentence.

1. **accolade** *(n.)* something given as a sign of approval, praise, or respect

   Her smile and thanks were _____ enough for me.

2. **desultory** *(adj.)* 1. lacking planning, order, or purpose; 2. random

   We spent the afternoon in _____ conversation.

3. **exorbitant** *(adj.)* 1. exceeding in intensity or quality; 2. too much

   They have spent _____ amounts of money fixing the kitchen.

4. **novice** *(n.)* a beginner; someone new at something

   Bill is really a _____ at sailing.

5. **pinnacle** *(n.)* 1. a high peak; 2. a pointed top, as of a mountain

   At the _____ of his career, he played the role of Hamlet.

Use Your Vocabulary—Challenge!

Award Speech The time has come to award the Great Big Prize to the citizen who has contributed the most to the well-being of the children of your community. Using the five Challenge Words above, write a speech awarding this year's Great Big Prize to a real or an imaginary person.

Vocabulary in Action

The word *desultory* (ca. 1581) comes from the Latin word *desultorius*. This is the adjective form of *desultur,* which means "hasty, casual, superficial." The word's noun form refers to "a rider in the circus who jumped from one horse to another while they are in gallop."

Ten vocabulary words are hidden in the puzzle below. Words may appear backward, forward, up, down, or diagonally. Find and circle all the words.

```
I  M  L  U  C  M  N  Y  T  T  R  I  L  I  G  E
J  C  G  N  I  O  G  O  Z  O  H  T  F  F  W  S
A  I  T  H  O  R  E  F  Y  G  O  L  O  C  E  I
C  P  D  C  E  G  S  N  D  N  T  O  F  I  M  M
K  O  Y  A  T  D  A  O  O  B  A  Y  M  E  O  O
L  T  A  K  E  E  L  R  N  S  H  V  U  E  X  R
Y  E  N  L  F  R  S  C  A  I  U  U  T  G  N  V
T  L  V  A  O  H  A  E  S  P  M  C  I  F  O  K
O  A  J  C  S  A  N  Q  R  R  B  T  C  I  R  E
A  Z  E  I  U  R  T  A  O  K  L  E  H  U  S  X
N  Z  O  H  R  C  V  B  Q  A  E  L  G  I  M  O
T  E  J  T  D  L  O  O  Y  C  J  M  O  B  I  B
I  B  C  Y  B  O  G  I  E  S  I  V  E  D  T  L
C  N  U  M  V  A  R  N  C  K  O  A  I  E  L  E
I  E  E  X  L  R  E  F  I  A  S  C  O  D  D  H
Z  B  L  E  Z  I  S  Y  L  B  A  I  N  E  L  S
```

Vocabulary in Action

Tycoon and *love* are two words not often associated with one another. But F. Scott Fitzgerald wrote a novel titled *The Love of The Last Tycoon*. The novel centers on the life of Hollywood film executive Monroe Stahr in the 1930s. Stahr's character is very loosely modeled on the life of film executive Irving Thalberg. Fitzgerald died suddenly, at age 45, leaving the book unfinished. The notes for the novel were collected and edited by literary critic Edmund Wilson, who was a close friend of Fitzgerald's. The unfinished novel was originally published in 1941 under the title *The Last Tycoon*.

WORD LIST

Read each word using the pronunciation key.

antithesis (an tith´ ə sis)
burly (bər´ lē)
crucial (krōō´ shəl)
devote (di vōt´)
disentangle (dis in taŋ´ gəl)
economic (e kə nom´ ic)
ethnic (eth´ nik)
fidelity (fi del´ i tē)
garish (gâr´ ish)
hurdle (hər´ dəl)
intervene (in tər vēn´)
literacy (lit´ ər ə sē)
naive (nī ēv´)
perimeter (pə rim´ i tər)
presumptuous (pri zump´ chōō əs)
reminisce (rem ə nis´)
siphon (sī´ fən)
sustain (sə stān´)
ultimate (ul´ tə mət)
zeal (zēl)

WORD STUDY

Analogies

Analogies show relationships between pairs of words. Study the relationships between the pairs of words below.

backpack is to **student** as **briefcase** is to **lawyer**

biology is to **doctor** as **math** is to **accountant**

lion is to **Africa** as **panda** is to **Asia**

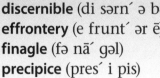
Challenge Words

abhor (ab hôr´)
discernible (di sərn´ ə bəl)
effrontery (e frunt´ ər ē)
finagle (fə nā´ gəl)
precipice (pres´ i pis)

© Loyola Press.

163

Level H

Read each sentence below to figure out the meaning of the word in **bold**. Use reasoning skills and the remainder of the sentence to help you. Write the meaning of the word on the line.

1. Should we **intervene** or let the group work out the problem on its own?

   _____

2. A metal fence ran along the **perimeter** of the park.

   _____

3. Good weather is **crucial** for the launching of the space shuttle.

   _____

4. Martina cleaned the chalkboard with such **zeal** that her teacher let her do it daily.

   _____

5. The town has severe **economic** problems; several businesses have closed in the last two months.

   _____

6. After law school, Patricia's **ultimate** goal is to become a Supreme Court justice.

   _____

7. One bowl of cereal will not **sustain** a growing child for a whole day.

   _____

8. The principal said that Kevin's yellow and purple suit was too **garish** to wear at graduation.

   _____

9. People value dogs as pets because of their **fidelity** to their owners.

   _____

10. I never thought she would be so **presumptuous** as to fix herself a sandwich in someone else's house.

   _____

WORD MEANINGS

Word Learning

Study the spelling, part(s) of speech, and meaning(s) of each word. Complete each sentence by writing the word on the line. Then read the sentence.

1. antithesis *(n.)* the direct opposite

Her idea is the _____ of everything we've worked for.

2. burly *(adj.)* 1. large in bodily size; 2. strongly built; 3. stout

We found a _____ police officer to help us lift the fallen tree.

3. crucial *(adj.)* vitally important or essential

You have forgotten one _____ point.

4. devote *(v.)* 1. to apply entirely to one activity; 2. to set aside for some purpose

Jeb decided to _____ all of his free time to practicing his tennis game.

5. disentangle *(v.)* to free from entanglement or complication

The turtle tried to _____ itself from the fishing net.

6. economic *(adj.)* having to do with the management and behavior of goods, services, and money

The country has reached an _____ crisis.

7. ethnic *(adj.)* of a particular religious, racial, national, or cultural group

You'll find a number of _____ restaurants on Macomb Street.

8. fidelity *(n.)* 1. loyalty; 2. faithfulness to obligations

His employers valued his _____ to the company.

9. garish *(adj.)* having excessively bright colors or decorations, gaudy

I don't much care for that _____ window display.

10. hurdle *(n.)* 1. a barrier used in foot races; 2. a problem that must be overcome; *(v.)* 1. to jump over a barrier; 2. to overcome a problem

Mark's brother cut his leg on a racing _____.

We watched the children _____ the fence.

11. intervene *(v.)* 1. to come between; to interfere; 2. to happen between two points of time

I didn't intend to _____, so I'll leave you two alone now.

12. **literacy** *(n.)* the ability to read and write

    Compared with many countries, the United States has a high rate of

    _____.

13. **naive** *(adj.)* 1. showing great simplicity; 2. without much knowledge of the world

    You say she's lived all over the world, but she appears so _____.

14. **perimeter** *(n.)* 1. the edge around a space; 2. the length of the edge around a space

    We planted daffodils and tulips around the _____ of the yard.

15. **presumptuous** *(adj.)* inappropriately bold or confident

    Would it be _____ of me to ask for a raise?

16. **reminisce** *(v.)* to remember or talk about past events

    My mom likes to visit with her sisters and _____ about their childhood.

17. **siphon** *(n.)* a curved pipe or tube used to move a liquid from one container to another; *(v.)* to take out by using a siphon

    You'll have to use a _____ to drain the tank.

    A long tube will _____ water from the basin.

18. **sustain** *(v.)* 1. to keep; to prolong; 2. to provide for

    I can't _____ this effort much longer.

19. **ultimate** *(adj.)* 1. final; 2. of the greatest size or importance; *(n.)* 1. the final point; 2. the greatest point

    At the top of the hill, she faced the _____ challenge.

    As an athlete, she strove for the _____.

20. **zeal** *(n.)* eager attention or enthusiasm for a cause or goal

    Lucas could not contain his _____ for writing stories.

Vocabulary in Action

The word **antithesis** (ca. 1529) comes from the Late Latin word *antithesis* (Greek "antithesis" or "opposition"). It literally means "a placing against."

Use Your Vocabulary

Choose the word from the Word List that best completes each sentence. Write the word on the line. You may use the plural form of nouns and the past tense of verbs if necessary.

Although the program had overcome other difficulties, Books Across Borders now faced its greatest __1__ ever. The organization worked to raise the level of __2__ across all __3__ groups and neighborhood lines in the city of Little Falls. Its __4__ to community values and sound teaching had earned it a very good reputation. Books Across Borders had volunteers who __5__ every weekend to distributing books and tutoring children and adults. These volunteers applied themselves to the task with __6__ ; they represented the __7__ of selfish city dwellers.

However, Joyce Balderas, the organization's leader, found that Books Across Borders faced serious __8__ trouble. A local company, which had always contributed a(n) __9__ portion of the group's annual budget, had just closed. Joyce was not so __10__ to think that enthusiasm alone would __11__ the organization.

Joyce walked around the __12__ of her tiny office, thinking of how to __13__ Books Across Borders from this financial trap. She hoped she would not have to __14__ money away from the tutorial programs in order to pay the rent. She __15__ aloud about the old days, when the organization did not even have an office but worked out of her dining room. Could they do without an office again?

Someone knocked on the door. She opened it to a __16__ man dressed in __17__ clothing.

"I don't mean to be __18__ , he said, "but I overheard you talking to yourself and I think I may have the __19__ answer to your problems." He said that he knew of several small companies that wanted to donate to the organization.

"Thank you so much!" Joyce said. "You have __20__ just in time!"

1. _____
2. _____
3. _____
4. _____
5. _____
6. _____
7. _____
8. _____
9. _____
10. _____
11. _____
12. _____
13. _____
14. _____
15. _____
16. _____
17. _____
18. _____
19. _____
20. _____

SYNONYMS

Synonyms are words that have the same or nearly the same meanings.

Part 1 Choose the word from the box that is the best synonym for each group of words. Write the word on the line.

burly	intervene	presumptuous	sustain
crucial	perimeter	reminisce	ultimate

1. recollect, remember _____

2. maintain, nurture, support _____

3. border, circumference, boundary _____

4. last, conclusive, utmost, peak _____

5. bold, overconfident, impertinent _____

6. step in, mediate, intercede _____

7. critical, significant, momentous _____

8. brawny, stocky, hefty _____

Part 2 Replace the underlined word with a word from the box that means the same or almost the same. Write your answer on the line.

garish	antithesis	hurdle	naive
ethnic	fidelity	zeal	

9. She performed the role with great <u>fervor</u>. _____

10. People of many different <u>national</u> groups lived in the neighborhood.

    _____

11. Jasmine knew that to become senator she'd have to overcome a great <u>obstacle</u>.

    _____

12. The two have always shown great <u>allegiance</u> to each other. _____

13. We are striving not for war but for its <u>opposite</u>. _____

14. Scott has a very <u>innocent</u> view of the world. _____

15. Whenever we have a party, Erika shows up in <u>flashy</u> clothing.

_____

ANTONYMS

Antonyms are words that have opposite or nearly opposite meanings.

Part 1 Choose the word from the box that is the best antonym for each group of words. Write the word on the line.

antithesis	fidelity	presumptuous
disentangle	perimeter	sustain

1. twin, equal, duplicate   _____

2. hesitant, insecure, unsure   _____

3. snare, catch, tie up   _____

4. center, middle, core   _____

5. discontinue, stop, let down   _____

6. falseness, treason, fickleness   _____

Part 2 Replace the underlined word with a word from the box that means the opposite or almost the opposite. Write your answer on the line.

garish	crucial	zeal
naive	burly	ultimate

7. Look at those <u>puny</u> arms! _____

8. The substitute teacher appears to be very <u>sophisticated</u>. _____

9. You have forgotten a few <u>trivial</u> details. _____

10. She wore a <u>plain</u> scarf around her neck. _____

11. My <u>initial</u> goal is to finish this assignment on time. _____

12. Hunter responded to every request with <u>indifference</u>. _____

WORD STUDY

Analogies To complete the following analogies, decide what kind of relationship is shown by the first pair of words. Then fill in the bubble next to the other pair of words that show the same relationship.

1. **big** is to **enormous** as
   - a. little is to huge
   - b. small is to tiny
   - c. right is to wrong
   - d. delicious is to sweet

2. **bulldozer** is to **construction** as
   - a. submarine is to war
   - b. hammer is to nail
   - c. horse is to training
   - d. ship is to sailor

3. **winter** is to **shiver** as
   - a. autumn is to sleep
   - b. night is to watch
   - c. evening is to follow
   - d. summer is to sweat

4. **curtain** is to **window** as
   - a. sheet is to bed
   - b. water is to faucet
   - c. melon is to knife
   - d. napkin is to crumb

5. **tooth** is to **comb** as
   - a. sand is to water
   - b. brick is to wall
   - c. paper is to computer
   - d. TV is to library

6. **apple** is to **fruit** as
   - a. fish is to fowl
   - b. ice cream is to milk
   - c. perch is to fish
   - d. tree is to oak

Vocabulary in Action

Many scientists believe that analogy plays a major role in problem solving, decision making, memory, creativity, emotion, and communication. Analogy lies behind basic tasks such as the identification of places, objects, and people. In fact, some scientists have argued that analogy is "the core of cognition."

CHALLENGE WORDS

Word Learning—Challenge!

Study the spelling, part of speech, and meaning of each word. Complete each sentence by writing the word on the line. Then read the sentence.

1. **abhor** *(v.)* to feel great hatred or disgust for

   I _____ the practice of cheating on tests.

2. **discernible** *(adj.)* able to be seen or perceived

   Her footprints were barely _____ in the drifting snow.

3. **effrontery** *(n.)* audacity; boldness

   I thought he showed great _____ in speaking to his elders that way.

4. **finagle** *(v.)* to get something by being tricky or clever

   Julia managed to _____ a couple of tickets to the game.

5. **precipice** *(n.)* a very steep cliff or overhanging place

   One lone bush grew atop the _____.

Use Your Vocabulary—Challenge!

Librarian's Lament You are a librarian at a local library. While you love books and working with people, you sometimes feel frustrated by patrons who show disrespect for the library, its books, or other patrons. Using the five Challenge Words above, write a diary entry explaining how you feel about your job.

> ### Notable Quotes
>
> "Most are engaged in business the greater part of their lives, because the soul **abhors** a vacuum and they have not discovered any continuous employment for man's nobler faculties."
>
> —Henry David Thoreau (1817–1862), American writer and philosopher

FUN WITH WORDS

You've just been hired by a local artist to name her new paintings. Below you'll find a description of each painting and a partial title. Fill in the blank in each title with the vocabulary word from this chapter that fits best.

1. This painting shows two boys using a tube to drain water from one bathtub to another. It's entitled "The _____."

2. The canvas of this painting is composed entirely of one-dollar bills. Name this one "A(n) _____ Foundation."

3. Only the outer edges of this piece have been painted. It's called "Living on the _____."

4. In this work, three flies try to save another fly who is caught in a spiderweb. Its title is "Hoping to _____ a Friend."

5. Two people are on a porch swing, watching the sunset and looking through an old photograph album. This painting's name is "A Good Time to _____."

6. Half of this painting is white, while the other half is completely black. Call this one "_____."

7. This painting shows two men standing together. Both men are more than 7 feet tall and each weighs nearly 300 pounds. It's called "The _____ Brothers."

8. In this painting, two children are holding the earth gently in their hands. Call it "Let's _____ Our World."

Review 13–15

Word Meanings Fill in the bubble of the word that is best defined by each phrase.

1. to mangle or disable
   - **a.** reiterate
   - **b.** mutilate
   - **c.** oscillate
   - **d.** discriminate

2. a silly act or caper
   - **a.** controversy
   - **b.** paragon
   - **c.** siphon
   - **d.** antic

3. capable of being read
   - **a.** legible
   - **b.** crucial
   - **c.** burly
   - **d.** durable

4. the maximum
   - **a.** reliability
   - **b.** ultimate
   - **c.** gale
   - **d.** subordination

5. showing great emotion
   - **a.** ethnic
   - **b.** inquisitive
   - **c.** fervent
   - **d.** ultimate

6. to regard or value highly
   - **a.** succumb
   - **b.** envelop
   - **c.** devote
   - **d.** esteem

7. overly bright or ornamented
   - **a.** brisk
   - **b.** mythical
   - **c.** garish
   - **d.** naive

8. the blockade of a town or fortress
   - **a.** siege
   - **b.** fiasco
   - **c.** perimeter
   - **d.** fury

9. a complete opposite
   - **a.** zeal
   - **b.** integral
   - **c.** fidelity
   - **d.** antithesis

10. capable of withstanding wear and tear
    - **a.** humble
    - **b.** durable
    - **c.** credible
    - **d.** amiable

11. a perfect example
    - **a.** paragon
    - **b.** buoy
    - **c.** predator
    - **d.** tycoon

12. to supply with needed nourishment
    - **a.** sustain
    - **b.** devise
    - **c.** detract
    - **d.** devote

13. heavy and strong
    - **a.** liable
    - **b.** fervent
    - **c.** burly
    - **d.** wretched

14. an adventure tale
    - **a.** yarn
    - **b.** siege
    - **c.** fiasco
    - **d.** hurdle

15. to recall the past
    - **a.** reminisce
    - **b.** disentangle
    - **c.** envelop
    - **d.** intervene

16. contempt or aggressive dislike
    - **a.** ecology
    - **b.** antic
    - **c.** literacy
    - **d.** hostility

17. legally obligated

    (a.) presumptuous   **(b.)** liable   **c.** inquisitive   **d.** ethnic

18. of the highest importance

    (a.) garish   **(b.)** crucial   **c.** brisk   **(d.)** preliminary

19. lack of harmony

    (a.) twinge   **(b.)** reliability   **c.** silhouette   **(d.)** discord

20. worthy of confidence

    (a.) economic   **(b.)** naive   **(c.)** credible   **(d.)** legible

Sentence Completion

Choose the word from the box that best completes each of the following sentences. Write the word in the blank.

fiasco	oscillates	amiable	tycoon	silhouettes
succumb	presumptuous	humble	gale	siphon

1. After oil was discovered on his farm, Jake became a petroleum _____ almost overnight.

2. We bought a fan that _____ on its base and blows air all across the room.

3. My father and I were able to _____ some gas from the car's tank into the lawn mower's tank.

4. Light from the candle cast eerie, flickering _____ of us onto the far wall.

5. The _____ senior was shocked to learn that he had not been elected homecoming king.

6. We knew that the play was a complete _____ when two of the props collapsed.

7. Even though she's now an international star, Katelyn has remained as _____ as ever.

8. We hope our parents _____ to our pleas to let us go to the beach.

9. Spending time with friends always puts me in a(n) _____ mood.

10. We secured the windows when the _____ began to grow stronger.

Fill in the Blanks Fill in the bubble of the pair of words that best completes each sentence.

1. The old sailor spun a(n) _____ about a _____ sea monster from an ancient legend.
   - (a.) fury, wretched
   - (b.) yarn, mythical
   - (c.) antic, garish
   - (d.) controversy, durable

2. Chuck had to _____ the _____ kitten from the vine it tried to climb.
   - (a.) disentangle, inquisitive
   - (b.) oscillate, legible
   - (c.) reminisce, mythical
   - (d.) detract, brisk

3. The _____ draft of my story is barely _____.
   - (a.) burly, presumptuous
   - (b.) crucial, humble
   - (c.) garish, mythical
   - (d.) preliminary, legible

4. My little sister is so _____ that she thinks that anything I tell her is _____.
   - (a.) naive, credible
   - (b.) burly, presumptuous
   - (c.) durable, crucial
   - (d.) fervent, economic

5. The volunteer's _____ for the cause makes her our most _____ worker.
   - (a.) siphon, mythical
   - (b.) twinge, inquisitive
   - (c.) zeal, fervent
   - (d.) perimeter, ultimate

6. The _____ between the two former best friends was so strong that their teacher felt she had to _____.
   - (a.) fidelity, discriminate
   - (b.) discord, intervene
   - (c.) buoy, detract
   - (d.) silhouette, reiterate

7. Gerry has overcome so many _____ that everyone holds her in high _____.
   - (a.) paragons, humble
   - (b.) predators, siege
   - (c.) tycoons, literacy
   - (d.) hurdles, esteem

8. The party turned into a(n) _____ after two guests displayed their _____.
   - (a.) antithesis, buoys
   - (b.) ecology, literacy
   - (c.) hurdle, reliability
   - (d.) fiasco, hostility

9. The club members gathered to _____ a plan to better their _____ situation by doing odd jobs.
   - (a.) devise, economic
   - (b.) mutilate, amiable
   - (c.) oscillate, integral
   - (d.) envelop, brisk

10. The clown's _____ costume is the _____ of beautiful.
    - (a.) wretched, tycoon
    - (b.) garish, antithesis
    - (c.) liable, ultimate
    - (d.) mythical, subordination

175

Level H   Review 13–15

Classifying Words

Sort the words in the box by writing each word to complete a phrase in the correct category.

amiable	controversy	devoted	disentangle	durable
envelops	ethnic	fidelity	garish	hostility
humble	mutilated	perimeter	reliability	reminisce
succumbs	sustained	twinge	wretched	zeal

Words You Might Use to Talk About Moods

1. cheerful and _____ every day
2. always so _____ even though she is very talented
3. scowling face makes him seem filled with _____
4. dives into every project with energy and _____
5. never _____ to unhappiness

Words You Might Use to Talk About Friendship

6. sympathy that _____ her the day her dog died
7. proves his _____ by keeping my secrets
8. can always be counted on for honesty and _____
9. _____ to everyone who has been kind to her
10. likes to _____ about our kindergarten days

Words You Might Use to Talk About Things That Go Wrong

11. a(n) _____ in my back from picking up the heavy suitcase
12. baby sister who _____ her brother's science report
13. _____ with Dad about cleaning our room
14. stop to _____ my hair from the bubble gum
15. feeling _____ because he has the flu

Words You Might Use to Talk About Clothing

16. favorite _____ costume for family holidays
17. fringe around the _____ of the hat's brim
18. comfortable, long-lasting, _____ jeans
19. a(n) _____ shirt with a big print in bright colors
20. hood that _____ my ears on cold days

NAME _____

Posttest

Choosing the Definitions Fill in the bubble next to the item that best defines the boldface word in each sentence.

1. The babysitter takes Lulu for a daily **jaunt** to the park.
   - (a.) jog
   - (b.) outing
   - (c.) ride
   - (d.) gate

2. Computers quickly become obsolete.
   - (a.) out-of-date
   - (b.) powerful
   - (c.) enjoyable
   - (d.) up-to-date

3. The police spotted the **fugitive** in front of the abandoned building.
   - (a.) older woman
   - (b.) stolen goods
   - (c.) car
   - (d.) runaway

4. The next week we all got together to **reminisce** about the dance.
   - (a.) wonder
   - (b.) forget
   - (c.) guess
   - (d.) remember

5. Some people blush and **stammer** when they are nervous.
   - (a.) perspire
   - (b.) fidget
   - (c.) stutter
   - (d.) relax

6. The absolute **minimum** Justin will sell the bike for is $20.
   - (a.) most
   - (b.) least
   - (c.) price
   - (d.) deal

7. Don't drink from that cup with a chip in its **brim**.
   - (a.) bottom
   - (b.) handle
   - (c.) edge
   - (d.) design

8. When the rescuers found the lost child, she was suffering from **dehydration**.
   - (a.) lack of water
   - (b.) lack of air
   - (c.) extreme heat
   - (d.) extreme cold

9. The forest ranger lives as a **recluse** for part of the year.
   - (a.) mountaineer
   - (b.) hermit
   - (c.) pioneer
   - (d.) firefighter

10. In the flickering light, I saw a strange **silhouette** on the wall.
    - (a.) painting
    - (b.) shadow
    - (c.) stain
    - (d.) curtain

11. That rude attitude is the **antithesis** of friendliness.
    - (a.) beginning
    - (b.) example
    - (c.) opposite
    - (d.) offspring

12. William Shakespeare achieved **immortality** through his plays.
    - (a.) lasting fame
    - (b.) beautiful poetry
    - (c.) large audiences
    - (d.) great wealth

13. Jocelyn had an **absurd** idea for a gift for our father.
    - (a.) brilliant
    - (b.) unique
    - (c.) reasonable
    - (d.) foolish

14. We won't give up until we've **exhausted** all our options.
    - (a.) considered
    - (b.) counted
    - (c.) used up
    - (d.) acted on

15. Paul acts as if losing the game is a huge **calamity**.
    - (a.) victory
    - (b.) disaster
    - (c.) disappointment
    - (d.) score

16. Cats have a reputation for being **finicky** eaters.
   a. picky   **b.** gluttonous   **c.** frequent   **d.** quiet

17. Before Stephen chose his new car, he **agonized** about the decision for weeks.
   a. worried   **b.** thought   **c.** cried   **d.** read

18. The **drone** of the air conditioner put Alora to sleep.
   a. cool air   **b.** clanking   **c.** breaking down   **d.** hum

19. The volunteers **itemized** the supplies to go in each kit.
   a. arranged   **b.** listed   **c.** distributed   **d.** hid

20. Julian's answer wasn't brilliant, but it was an **admissible** response.
   a. bold   **b.** uncertain   **c.** incorrect   **d.** acceptable

21. Accuracy on the test is more important than speed.
   a. thinking   **b.** handwriting   **c.** correctness   **d.** attitude

22. If we sit on the **knoll**, we'll have a view of the whole park.
   a. stool   **b.** ground   **c.** hill   **d.** ledge

23. The group met to decide how to **allocate** the money the car wash raised.
   a. distribute   **b.** spend   **c.** invest   **d.** count

24. On every holiday, our family gets together for a **bounteous** meal.
   a. spicy   **b.** plentiful   **c.** delicious   **d.** shared

25. Cracking her knuckles is my cousin's most annoying **quirk**.
   a. noise   **b.** feeling   **c.** pest   **d.** habit

26. Ethan is fascinated by musicians, painters, and others of that **ilk**.
   a. origin   **b.** type   **c.** opinion   **d.** belief

27. The first football practice was a real **fiasco**.
   a. comedy   **b.** success   **c.** failure   **d.** party

28. I planted a **multitude** of flowers, but only a few came up.
   a. variety   **b.** garden   **c.** bouquet   **d.** vast number

29. Jordan never had an **inkling** that her friends were planning a surprise party.
   a. doubt   **b.** concern   **c.** hint   **d.** reminder

30. Which candidate do you plan to **endorse**?
   a. watch   **b.** approve   **c.** vote for   **d.** campaign against

Word Relations

Word Relations Synonyms are words that have the same or nearly the same meanings. Antonyms are words that have the opposite or nearly the opposite meanings. In the blank before each pair of words, write *S* if the words are synonyms, *A* if they are antonyms, or *N* if they are not related.

1. _____ fluted   sedate
2. _____ emotional   stoic
3. _____ inquisitive   unintelligible
4. _____ controversy   siege
5. _____ aspiration   sequence
6. _____ upkeep   upheaval
7. _____ squelch   sustain
8. _____ laud   esteem
9. _____ isolate   secrete
10. _____ pivot   oscillate
11. _____ dismay   jollity
12. _____ facet   component
13. _____ tranquil   irascible
14. _____ endeavor   subordination
15. _____ burly   gaunt

16. _____ afflicted   indifferent
17. _____ detract   exert
18. _____ crucial   fundamental
19. _____ frail   tangible
20. _____ fury   tumult
21. _____ fatigued   weary
22. _____ amiable   belligerent
23. _____ optical   opaque
24. _____ benign   ferocious
25. _____ catastrophe   calamity
26. _____ jaunt   excursion
27. _____ lithe   luminous
28. _____ inadequate   admissible
29. _____ finite   fiasco
30. _____ agitate   stimulate

Using Context Clues

Using Context Clues Fill in the bubble next to the phrase that best completes each sentence.

1. Savannah hoped the man was **acquitted** because
   (a.) she believed he was innocent.   (c.) she believed he was guilty.
   (b.) he didn't like his job.   (d.) she wanted his job.

2. **Literacy** is important when you are
   (a.) eating dinner.   (c.) doing someone a favor.
   (b.) exercising.   (d.) filling out a job application.

3. Tom **endeared** himself to Jenny by
   (a.) being kind to her.   (c.) avoiding her.
   (b.) ridiculing her.   (d.) moving next door to her.

4. A **pillar** is usually used to
- (a.) remove skin from a vegetable.
- (c.) remove a splinter.
- (b.) support a roof.
- (d.) take a nap.

5. If you have **tenacity**, you have
- (a.) flexibility.
- (c.) determination.
- (b.) fear.
- (d.) an upset stomach.

6. Those who **persist** in a task
- (a.) will never finish it.
- (c.) will most likely finish it.
- (b.) will be scolded.
- (d.) will be rewarded.

7. A **buoy** is usually
- (a.) in the water.
- (c.) on a mountainside.
- (b.) tied to a tree.
- (d.) hard to see.

8. A **rascal** is known for his or her
- (a.) magic tricks.
- (c.) bravery.
- (b.) seriousness.
- (d.) unruly behavior.

9. Will's **elimination** from the spelling bee
- (a.) earned him a trophy.
- (c.) was in Monday's newspaper.
- (b.) left only three contestants.
- (d.) made him very proud.

10. If you are **liable** for the damage, you
- (a.) are sorry for it.
- (c.) are responsible for it.
- (b.) are angry about it.
- (d.) have lied about it.

11. The **ultimate** letter in the alphabet is
- (a.) the first one.
- (c.) the least common one.
- (b.) the most common one.
- (d.) the last one.

12. Elena has **devoted** herself to the project because she
- (a.) doesn't have time for it.
- (c.) believes it is an important one.
- (b.) has lost interest in it.
- (d.) isn't sure whom she will vote for.

13. Your argument is so **persuasive** that
- (a.) I have changed my mind.
- (c.) nobody will listen to it.
- (b.) I can't believe what you say.
- (d.) you will surely offend someone.

14. He acted as an **accessory** to the theft by
- (a.) arresting the criminal.
- (c.) calling the police.
- (b.) helping the thief escape.
- (d.) distracting the thief.

15. You may want to **envelop** the baby in a
(a.) blanket.
(b.) bonnet.
(c.) bathtub.
(d.) playpen.

16. We questioned the car's **reliability**
(a.) when we painted it.
(b.) because it had no radio.
(c.) when it wouldn't start.
(d.) because we wanted to sell it.

17. A person demonstrates **fidelity** by
(a.) playing a musical instrument.
(b.) acting in a play.
(c.) keeping promises.
(d.) breaking promises.

18. Ariana took a **brisk** walk around the block because
(a.) she had plenty of time.
(b.) she didn't have much time.
(c.) she was recovering from an illness.
(d.) she was tired.

19. You are **entitled** to enter the theater if you
(a.) try to sneak in the back door.
(b.) have purchased a ticket.
(c.) don't like horror movies.
(d.) have forgotten your money.

20. In **defiance** of the law, Jon
(a.) read a book about lawyers.
(b.) stopped at every red light.
(c.) voted in every election.
(d.) sped through the stop sign.

21. You may be **astounded** when
(a.) a red light turns green.
(b.) leaves begin to sprout in the spring.
(c.) your friends give you a surprise party.
(d.) your favorite TV show airs each week.

22. Animals that **forage** are
(a.) trotting along.
(b.) playing together.
(c.) looking for a home.
(d.) searching for food.

23. If you dream of leading a **monarchy**, you wish you could
(a.) be a king or a queen.
(b.) migrate with butterflies.
(c.) be at the head of a parade.
(d.) live the life of a recluse.

24. If you are frightened by a **gale**, you are
(a.) scared of a small girl.
(b.) locked inside a fence.
(c.) caught in a storm.
(d.) lost at the zoo.

25. An **optimistic** person
(a.) has a gloomy outlook.
(b.) looks for good things in life.
(c.) has a new pair of glasses.
(d.) is standing on a hill.

Analogies
Analogies show relationships between pairs of words.

To complete the analogies, decide what kind of relationship is shown by the first pair of words. Then fill in the bubble next to the other pair of words that show the same relationship.

1. **saline** is to **ocean** as
   - (a.) punishment is to strict
   - (b.) lengthy is to brief
   - (c.) sour is to lemon
   - (d.) caustic is to praise

2. **flippant** is to **respectful** as
   - (a.) harmful is to beneficial
   - (b.) scholar is to studious
   - (c.) average is to mediocre
   - (d.) engine is to powerful

3. **credible** is to **believable** as
   - (a.) engaged is to occupied
   - (b.) forever is to infinite
   - (c.) worrisome is to problem
   - (d.) persuade is to convince

4. **commencement** is to **beginning** as
   - (a.) queen is to monarchy
   - (b.) gale is to moan
   - (c.) perimeter is to boundary
   - (d.) argument is to intervene

5. **empty** is to **bucket** as
   - (a.) conceal is to display
   - (b.) scold is to compliment
   - (c.) deflate is to tire
   - (d.) snare is to trap

6. **accident** is to **haphazard** as
   - (a.) casual is to nonchalant
   - (b.) lamp is to luminous
   - (c.) ambitious is to lazy
   - (d.) trivia is to significant

7. **scrutinize** is to **skim** as
   - (a.) wonder is to mystery
   - (b.) decry is to criticize
   - (c.) alarm is to comfort
   - (d.) respond is to reply

8. **squander** is to **waste** as
   - (a.) savory is to meal
   - (b.) stash is to spend
   - (c.) splinter is to board
   - (d.) plunder is to steal

9. **encounter** is to **random** as
   - (a.) curiosity is to knowledge
   - (b.) maneuver is to skillful
   - (c.) feat is to accomplishment
   - (d.) bilk is to cheat

10. **disown** is to **reject** as
    - (a.) secure is to loosen
    - (b.) charge is to drain
    - (c.) free is to acquit
    - (d.) grief is to mourn

Test-Taking Tips

Taking a standardized test can be tough. Here are a few things you can do to make the experience easier.

Get a good night's sleep the night before the test. You want to be alert and rested in the morning.

Eat a healthful breakfast. Your brain needs good food to work properly.

Wear layers of clothing. You can take off or put on a layer if you get too warm or too cold.

Have two sharp number 2 pencils—with erasers—ready.

When you get the test, read the directions carefully. Be sure you understand what you are supposed to do. If you have any questions, ask your teacher before you start marking your answers.

If you feel nervous, close your eyes and take a deep breath as you silently count to three. Then slowly breathe out. Do this several times until your mind is calm.

Manage your time. Check to see how many questions there are. Try to answer half the questions before half the time is up.

Answer the easy questions first. If you don't know the answer to a question, skip it and come back to it later.

Try to answer all the questions. Some will seem very hard, but don't worry about it. Nobody is expected to get every answer right. Make the best guess you can.

If you make a mistake, erase it completely. Then write the correct answer or fill in the correct circle.

When you have finished, go back over the test. Work on any questions you skipped. Check your answers.

Question Types

Many tests contain the same kinds of questions. Here are a few question types you may encounter.

Meaning from Context

This kind of question asks you to figure out the meaning of a word from the words or sentences around it.

The smoke from the smoldering garbage made her eyes water.

Which word in the sentence helps you understand the meaning of *smoldering*?

smoke	garbage
eyes	water

Read the sentence carefully. You know that smoke comes from something that is burning. *Smoldering* must mean "burning." *Smoke* is the correct answer.

Synonyms and Antonyms

Some questions ask you to identify the synonym of a word. Synonyms are words that mean the same. Some questions ask you to identify the antonym of a word. Antonyms are words that mean the opposite.

> The workers buffed the statue until it shone like a mirror.

Which word is a synonym for *buffed*?

polished   covered

tarnished   dismantled

Read the answers carefully. Which word means "to make something shine?" The answer is *polish*.

> When she feels morose, she watches funny cartoons to change her mood.

Which word is an antonym of *morose*?

dismal   agreeable

happy   confident

Think about the sentence. If something funny will change her mood, she must be sad. The answer is *happy*, the antonym of sad.

Analogies

This kind of question asks you to find relationships between pairs of words. Analogies usually use *is to* and *as*.

> **Green** is to **grass** as _____ is to **sky**.

Green is the color of grass. So the answer must be **blue**, the color of sky.

Roots

Roots are the building blocks of words. Many roots come from ancient languages, such as Latin and Greek. If you know what a root means, you can often guess the meaning of a word. Some words are built by adding prefixes and suffixes to a root. Some words are formed by joining more than one root. Note that the spelling of a root can change. Some roots can stand alone as English words.

Root	Language	Meaning	Examples
act, ag	Latin	do, drive	action, agile
ann	Latin	year	anniversary, annual
cardi	Latin	heart	cardiologist, cardiogram
civ	Latin	citizen	civilian, civility
cred	Latin	believe	credulous, incredible
dent	Latin	tooth	denture, dentist
fid	Latin	faith	fidelity, confide
fract	Latin	break	fraction, fracture
gen	Greek	born	genesis, regenerate
grat	Latin	pleasing	gratuity, grateful
hydr	Greek	water	hydrant, hydraulic
imag	Latin	likeness	image, imagination
ject	Latin	throw	inject, reject
lat	Latin	side	lateral, bilateral
leg	Latin	law	legal, legislate
lit, liter	Latin	letters	literature, literary
loc	Latin	place	local, location
log	Greek	word, study	logic, dialogue, biology
mar	Latin	sea	marine, maritime
mech	Greek	machine	mechanic, mechanism
migr	Latin	move	migrate, immigrant

Root	Language	Meaning	Examples
nov	Latin	new	renovate, novitiate
pater	Latin	father	paternity, patrimony
rupt	Latin	break	erupt, interrupt
sign	Latin	mark	signature, signal
son	Latin	sound	consonant, resonate
spec	Latin	look, see	spectator, expect
tempo	Latin	time	temporary, extemporize
terra	Latin	earth	territory, terrain
tox	Latin	poison	intoxicate, toxin
urb	Latin	city	urban, suburb
ven	Latin	come	convene, convention
voc	Latin	call	vocal, evocative

Prefixes

A prefix is one or more syllables added to the beginning of a word to change its meaning.

Prefix	Meaning	Examples
aero-	air	aerospace
extra-	beyond	extraordinary
hyper-	excessive	hypersensitive
il-, in-, ir	not	illegible, inactive, irregular
mega-	large	megavitamin
mono-	one	monoculture, monorail
multi-	many, much	multipurpose, multiword
nano-	one billionth	nanosecond
out-	surpassing	outbid, outdo
tele-	distant	teleconference
trans-	across, beyond	transact

Suffixes

Suffixes

A suffix is one or more syllables added to the end of a word to change its meaning or to change it do a different part of speech.

Verb Suffixes

Suffix	Meaning	Examples
-ate	make	necessitate
-en	cause to be	deepen
-ify	make	beautify
-ize	cause to be	legalize

Noun Suffixes

Suffix	Meaning	Examples
-ance, -ancy, -ence, -ion, -ity, -ment, -ness, -ship, -ity	a state of being	vigilance, infancy, turbulence, explanation, generosity, assignment, kindness, kinship, modesty
-ant, -ent, -er, -or, -ist	one who	attendant, resident, hitter, actor, chemist

Adjective Suffixes

Suffix	Meaning	Examples
-able, -ible	capable of being	enjoyable, divisible
-ful	characterized by	careful
-less	without	useless
-y	like	thirsty

Adverb Suffix

Suffix	Meaning	Examples
-ly	like, resembling	quickly

Roots, Prefixes, and Suffixes

1. How does a hyperactive child behave?

   _____

2. His story sounded credible. How did it sound?

   _____

3. The woman went into cardiac arrest. What part of her body was affected?

   _____

4. His speech sounded very mechanical. How did it sound?

   _____

5. Where would an extraterrestrial come from?

   _____

6. What is a toxic substance?

   _____

7. What would you clean with a dentifrice?

   _____

8. Left turns are illegal at that corner. Why shouldn't you turn left there?

   _____

9. What do migratory animals do every year?

   _____

10. Who is your paternal grandfather?

    _____

11. What do spectacles help you do?

    _____

12. How long does it take for a tree to grow an annual ring?

    _____

13. What does an ape do when it vocalizes?

    _____

14. When you temporize, what are you trying to gain?

    _____

15. What kind of waves does sonar use to detect underwater objects?

    _____

16. Where is a maritime province located?

    _____

17. Whose rights do civil laws protect?

    _____

18. What kind of energy creates hydroelectricity?

    _____

19. What do you do when you gratify someone?

    _____

20. In what direction does a quarterback throw a lateral pass?

   _____

21. What does a literary critic write about?

   _____

22. What does an interurban train run between?

   _____

23. What does an infidel lack?

   _____

24. What is a monologue?

   _____

25. What does a locator do?

   _____

26. You put a pencil in a glass of water. How does refraction affect what you see?

   _____

27. The ruptured pipe caused the basement to flood. What happened to the pipe?

   _____

28. What is a characteristic of a multi-venue celebration?

   _____

29. What is the most remarkable thing about an innovation?

   _____

30. The superhero's car has an ejector seat. What does it do?

   _____

Word Cube

Categories: *Partners, Visual Learners*

Work with a partner. You will each need a sheet of paper, a pencil, tape, and a pair of scissors. Each of you chooses six of the current chapter's vocabulary words and makes a Word Cube. To make a Word Cube, draw six squares in a shape like this on the paper.

Write in each square one of the vocabulary words you chose. Then cut along the outside lines. Fold and tape the sides of the shape to make a cube. Take turns rolling the cubes. To score a point, write a sentence that makes sense, using the two words that were rolled. The first player to get five points wins the game.

Vocabulary Commercials

Categories: *Small Group, Technology*

Work with two partners. You will need several sheets of paper and a pencil. On one sheet of paper, list the vocabulary words from the current chapter. Then make a list of things you use every day—a bowl, cereal, shoes, and so on. Choose one of the items you listed and write a TV commercial to advertise that product. Write a script that lets all three partners play a role. Use at least 10 of the vocabulary words from the current chapter in your commercial. Practice acting out your commercial. Share your commercial with the class by making a video or by presenting a skit.

Creating Categories

Category: *Small Group*

Find two partners. You will each need a sheet of paper and a pencil. Each partner writes three of the current chapter's vocabulary words that are related in some way. For example, you might list words that are all used to describe people, that are all nouns, or that all describe ways to move from place to place. Challenge your partners to guess the connection between the words you listed.

Conducting Interviews

Categories: *Partners, Technology*

Work with a partner. You will need a sheet of paper and a pencil. One partner will be a news reporter and interview the other. The reporter writes questions to ask in the interview. The questions should contain at least 10 of the vocabulary words from the current chapter. The person being interviewed answers the questions, using vocabulary words if possible. When the interview is complete, switch places and let the other partner write questions and conduct an interview. If possible, record your interview on audio or video to share with the class.

Crack the Number Code

Categories: *Partners, ELL*

With a partner, write 10 sentences using the current chapter's vocabulary words. Next, assign a number to each letter of the alphabet (A=1, B=2, C=3, and so on). Code all the words in your sentences with the numbers you have assigned. For example, the code for the sentence "The cat sat on a mat" would be the following:

20, 8, 5 + 3, 1, 20 + 19, 1, 20 + 15, 14 + 1 + 13, 1, 20

Once you have coded all the sentences, exchange papers with another group and try to "crack the code." The first team to figure out all the sentences wins the game.

Crossword Puzzle

Categories: *Individual, Visual Learners*

Prepare for the game by bringing to class crossword puzzles from newspapers or magazines. Use these examples as a guide to create a crossword puzzle using the current chapter's vocabulary words. The word clues for "across" and "down" will be the vocabulary word definitions. Use graph paper for the crossword grid.

When finished, exchange puzzles with a friend and complete it. Return the crossword puzzle to its owner to check for accuracy.

Vocabulary Board Games

Categories: *Partners, Visual Learners*

Find a partner and discuss types of board games you like to play. Talk about the object of the game, the rules, and the equipment needed. Then create a Vocabulary Board Game. Think of a way to include the current chapter's vocabulary words in the game. For example, the vocabulary words could be written on word cards. When a player lands on a certain square, he or she must draw a card and define the word.

Create a game board on an open manila folder. Find or make game pieces, and write a list of game rules. Exchange Vocabulary Board Games with classmates and play their games. Keep the board games in a designated spot in the classroom and adapt the vocabulary cards for each new chapter.

All About Alliteration

Category: *Small Group*

Alliteration is the repetition of initial sounds within a sentence. Work in groups of three or four to create alliterative sentences that contain the current chapter's vocabulary words. The only words that can be used that do not start with the initial letter are *and, in, of, the, a,* and *an.* The object of the game is to see which group can come up with the longest sentence. (It can be silly, but it must make sense.) For example, using the vocabulary word *timid:*

The tremendously timid tiger tossed twelve tasteless trees toward the terrified turtle.

Word Sorts

Categories: *Small Group,*
Visual Learners

Work with a partner. Divide a sheet of paper into four sections labeled *Nouns, Adjectives, Adverbs,* and *Verbs.* Write each of the current chapter's vocabulary words in the appropriate section. When you and your partner feel that you have successfully placed each word in the appropriate box, turn your activity sheet upside down. (Allow only three minutes to complete this step.)

When the time has elapsed, exchange activity sheets with another pair and check for accuracy. (Use your *Vocabulary in Action* book for clarification.) The pair of partners with the most correct answers wins the game.

For an additional challenge, change the part of speech of the vocabulary words by using prefixes and suffixes. For example, if the vocabulary word is *migration,* you could add the verb *migrate* and the adjective *migratory.*

Good News, Bad News

Categories: *Individual,*
Partner

Write a good news and bad news letter to a friend or relative. Alternate sentences that begin "The good news is" with sentences that begin "The bad news is." Use one of the current chapter's vocabulary words in each "good news" sentence. Use an antonym of that vocabulary word in the "bad news" sentence. For example, if the word is *compliment,* you might write "The good news is I received a compliment from my teacher for doing a nice job on my research paper. The bad news is I gave my teacher an insult when I forgot to say "thank you."

For an extra challenge, leave blank spaces for the antonyms and exchange papers with a friend to complete.

Proofread Pen Pals

Category: *Small Group*

Find a friend and work together to write a friendly letter that includes at least six of the current chapter's vocabulary words. Your letter can be about school, sports, friends, family, or any other interesting topic. (Use a resource book to help you with the correct form for a friendly letter.) Include errors in your letter, such as spelling, punctuation, capitalization, and word meaning.

When you have completed your letter, exchange it with another pair of partners. Correct the new letter. After all the corrections have been made, return the letter to the original owners. They will make sure all the errors have been found.

Vocabulary Dominoes

Categories: *Small Group,*
ELL

Begin the game by writing all the current chapter's vocabulary words on index cards. Write the definitions of the words on other index cards.

Place all the index cards facedown in the center of the playing area. This will be the domino bank. Each player chooses four dominoes as his or her supply. Turn one domino faceup to begin play. The object of the game is to match the words with their definitions.

If Player 1 makes a match, he or she places the two cards down on the table, and Player 2 chooses. If Player 1 doesn't make a match, he or she must take a new domino from the bank. If that domino doesn't match either, the player must add it to his or her supply. Player 2 then tries to make a match. The first player to match all the dominoes in his or her supply is the winner.

Impromptu Stories

Category: *Small Group*

Write each of the current chapter's vocabulary word on an index card. Shuffle the cards and place them facedown in a deck. Players take turns drawing five cards from the deck. As each player draws cards, he or she makes up a story using the words on the five cards. Players can use any form of the word listed. To make the activity more challenging, try to make the players' stories build on one another.

Vocabulary Sayings

Category: *Small Group*

Find three partners. Write down the following five sayings:

Birds of a feather flock together.

A rolling stone gathers no moss.

Too many cooks spoil the broth.

A penny saved is a penny earned.

A stitch in time saves nine.

Then brainstorm other sayings. When your list is complete, rewrite the ending of each saying, using a vocabulary word from the current chapter. Example: Birds of a feather sit on our overhang.

Try to create two new endings for each saying. Share your list with other groups or create a class bulletin-board display of your work.

One-Sided Phone Conversations

Categories: *Small Group, Auditory Learners*

Find a partner. Work together to write one person's side of a phone conversation. Use at least 10 vocabulary words from the current chapter. Be sure to include both questions and answers in the conversation. When you have finished, find another pair of students with whom to work. Read your one-sided conversation to the other pair. After you read each sentence or question, ask them to fill in what the person on the other side of the conversation might have said. Then listen to the other pair's conversation and do the same. Try to use vocabulary words as you create the second side of the phone conversation.

Mystery Word Web

Categories: *Small Group, Visual Learners*

Find three partners. Draw a word web on a sheet of paper or on the board. One partner chooses a vocabulary word from the current chapter and fills in the outer circles of the web with clues about the word. The other partners try to guess which word is being suggested. Each partner should take at least two turns describing a word. Be sure to include the Challenge Words in the activity.

Vocabulary Answer and Question

Category: *Large Group*

Gather these materials: poster board, 20 index cards, a list of the current chapter's vocabulary words and definitions, tape. Tape the tops of the index cards to the poster board so that they form five columns of four cards. Under each index card, write a vocabulary word. Divide into two teams and line up in two rows facing each other. Flip a coin to see which team goes first.

The first player chooses and removes an index card, revealing the word beneath it. The team has 20 seconds to provide the definition of the word in question form. For example, if the word *usurp* is revealed, a correct response would be "What is 'to seize power from an individual or a group'?" If a correct definition is given, the team scores a point and the next player in line takes a turn. If an incorrect definition is given, play passes to the other team. The first person in line chooses a new index card. Play continues until all the cards have been removed. The team that gives the greater number of correct definitions wins.

Dictionary Dash

Category: *Small Group*

Find three partners and divide into two teams. You will need a dictionary, a sheet of paper, and a pencil. Write 10 vocabulary words on index cards and place them facedown on the floor. The first team turns over a card to reveal one of the vocabulary words. Each team should then look up the word in the dictionary and record the following

information about the vocabulary word on a sheet of paper:

how many different definitions the word has

the correct pronunciation

the guide words located on the dictionary page

a sentence that uses the word correctly

When both teams have finished, exchange papers and check for accuracy. The team that finishes first and has no mistakes receives two points. If the other team makes no mistakes, it receives one point. The game continues until all vocabulary index cards have been turned over. The team with the most points wins the game.

Vocabulary Haiku

Category: *Individual*

The word *haiku* comes from two Japanese words that mean "play" and "poem." A haiku is a poem that contains 17 syllables. It is written in a three-line format. The first line has five syllables, the second has seven syllables, and the third has five syllables. Frequently, a haiku describes a scene in nature.

Using the current chapter's vocabulary words, create your own haiku. For example, here is a haiku for the vocabulary word *harmonize*:

Soft falling raindrops
Harmonize with the children
Playing in the rain.

When the class has created several haiku, collect them and create a book. You may also wish to read your poems aloud to the class.

Word Wizards

Category: *Small Group*

Find three partners and divide into two teams. Choose one of the current chapter's vocabulary words. Each pair of partners writes the word at the top of a sheet of paper. The object of the game is to write as many forms of the word as possible by adding prefixes, suffixes, and word endings. For example, using the word *scribe,* you could write these words: *scriber, scribing, script, prescribe, subscription, subscribed, scribed, subscriber, subscript, subscribes, subscribe, subscribing.*

Each round should last three minutes. At the completion of a round, teams exchange papers and check for accuracy. Use a dictionary to clarify any questions.

For each correct word form, one point is awarded. For example, the above list would receive 12 points. Use a new vocabulary word for each round. The team with the most points at the end wins.

Captions

Categories: *Small Group, Visual Learners*

Find two partners. You will need old newspapers or magazines, scissors, paper, and glue or tape. Clip five pictures from the newspapers or magazines. Write a caption for each picture that describes what is being shown. Include at least one vocabulary word from the current chapter in each caption. Attach the captions to the photos and display them in the room.

Vocabulary Charades

Categories: *Small Group, Kinesthetic Learners*

Find three partners. Write on a slip of paper each vocabulary word from the current chapter. Fold the slips and drop them into a box. Partners take turns selecting words and acting them out. The actor may not make any sounds. The first person to guess the word earns a point.

Password

Category: *Small Group*

Find three partners and divide into two pairs. Write on a slip of paper each vocabulary word from a chapter. Divide the slips evenly between the teams. One partner will be the "giver" and the other the "receiver." The giver views the word on the first slip and gives the receiver a one-word clue about it. The receiver tries to guess the word. If he or she is correct, the giver goes to the next slip of paper. If the receiver is wrong, the giver gives another one-word clue. If the receiver does not guess the word after three clues, the giver goes to the next word. The team has three minutes to cover as many words as possible. A point is awarded for each correct answer. The second team then has three minutes to go through its words.

Pledges

Categories: *Partners, Visual Learners*

Work with a partner. Think of ways to improve your school or community. Write a pledge that lists the things you will do to make improvements. Use vocabulary words from the current chapter. Make an illustrated bulletin board of class pledges.

Here is a list of all the words defined in this book. The number following each word indicates the page on which the word is defined. The Challenge Words are listed in *italics*. The Word Study words are listed in **bold**.

Index of Words   Level H